DAMON HILL'S
CHAMPIONSHIP YEAR

Damon Hill's Championship Year

Bob McKenzie

HEADLINE

First published in 1996
by HEADLINE BOOK PUBLISHING

10 9 8 7 6 5 4 3 2

ISBN 0 7472 5599 7

Typeset by Avon Dataset Ltd, Bidford-on-Avon, Warks

Printed and bound in Great Britain by
Cox & Wyman Ltd, Reading, Berks

HEADLINE BOOK PUBLISHING
A division of Hodder Headline PLC
338 Euston Road
London NW1 3BH

Contents

1	A Time To Move On	1
2	A Slick Start	11
3	Rainman	29
4	Hill's Hat-Trick	41
5	Hill Loses His Grip	53
6	Hill Hits Back	63
7	Tunnel Vision	75
8	Hill Washed Out	91
9	Hill Robs Prodigal Son	103
10	Advantage Hill	115
11	Copse Corners Hill	125
12	Seven Up!	141
13	Disgust And Defeat	151
14	Radio Daze	159
15	Good Morning . . . Goodbye	169
16	Party Time – For Jacques	187
17	Glory Day	199

Acknowledgements

I would like to thank Nick Harris of ICN for supplying many of the pictures used in this book. Thanks also to the *Express* picture desk for their help, and to Empics.

1

A Time To Move On

Angry Atlantic rollers rose high and white out of the darkness, frozen in the light pouring from the picture windows of the restaurant, crashing their way to rocks outside as Damon Hill spoke of the relentless forces urging him on.

The dining establishments on the coast road out of Cascais on the royal coast which runs from Lisbon through Estoril are inviting havens of peace and plenitude at any time but one was even more delightful than usual on a Tuesday night in February. While most of Europe was in the grip of winter competitions, football and rugby tournaments, skiing and skating, Damon Hill was beginning the public preparation of his Formula One challenge, an eight-month chase of the sun across the globe.

It had been a sunny Portuguese day with the usual edge to a wind which had now picked up as night brought quiet to the Grand Prix circuit where eight teams had gathered to publicly test their cars which had been redesigned for the coming season. Inside, the warmth of the occasion, a select get-together, was helped by the superb seafood and wine and the company of Hill, who welcomed a break from a heavy schedule of test driving. He was in fine form, a man at peace with himself and the world and the craik, as the Irish call it, was in full flow for there were tales galore of the family move to a beautiful home near Dublin, which had taken place midway through 1995 but had now been completed.

There was the story of the one-armed glazier who came to measure a window and the resultant interesting shenanigans, his light-hearted worries that his sons were now saying 'dis' and 'dat' and 'tree' for this, that and three. Could this be the man whom some in his own team had named Mr Glum, who became known for his dark countenance, invoking the oft-repeated phrase: 'I wish he would smile more'?

A small group had gathered at the Panoramic restaurant at the request of Hill and around a table, in the out-of-season quietness, he laid out his new strategy which he believed would help him concentrate his energies to win the world drivers' championship.

Twice that title had been denied him by Michael Schumacher in successive years filled with controversy, punctuated by collisions between the two and comments which had led the world to believe that one would rather walk than share the last camel out of the Sahara with the other.

There were those who believed that having been beaten to the championship two years running by the brilliant German, the quieter, English family man would be a fractured case if not a broken man. The public perception of him was certainly of a gallant whinger, a moody, unsmiling, grafting competitor who was not destined to follow in the footsteps of his famous father, Graham, who twice had won the world championship. It was a sentiment Hill recognised and now, in Portugal, he was unveiling the 1996 model, revamped, restructured, re-vitalised after a winter of content, a season of shifting some of the furniture of life.

He looked fitter and leaner and this was a by-product of having a physiotherapist-trainer who had now been hired by the Rothmans Williams Renault team. Austrian Erwin Gollner had been taken on to help Hill and their new driver, 25-year-old French-Canadian Jacques Villeneuve. Hill counted him among his new supportive team which now surrounded him. He had appointed an image consultant, a public relations consultant, a commercial manager, and his lawyer Michael Breen was to take a more high-profile role during the season while his sister Brigitte would be manning their office.

'I realise now that while I have been trying to do everything myself with a few people helping,' said Hill, 'it would simplify things if we spread the load. I cannot tackle everything on my own. I have always been my own man, and that will continue, but now I accept that I need this outside help because there is so much to do off the track which can get in the way of focusing on racing.

'Don't forget, I have had only three full seasons and I have been pretty busy with driving so it is only now that I found it necessary to have others to do things for me.

'I have never thought that I needed anyone to collect my bag off the airport carousel and I don't see that changing, but there are things which now have to be handled by others.'

Hill's own high profile, his fan club and merchandising firm, demands for interviews from a vast range of newspapers, television, magazines and radio throughout the world have finally convinced him that time was too precious. He denied that it was also because the 1996 season was make-or-break but a candid view of the landscape around him was enough to convince most observers that it was this year or bust for a variety of reasons.

Nothing but the best would be good enough to earn Hill the title and, almost certainly as a result, a renewed and much enhanced contract with Williams. He would be 36 years old by the end of his fourth full season, his second as senior driver, and another runners-up prize would surely be too much for Frank Williams, a pragmatic man who would not take kindly to missing out on the drivers' championship for a third successive year.

The contenders were few, too, even at this early stage of the year. Schumacher had finally divorced from Benetton, who had built their team around him since signing him in 1991. He had been lured by Formula One's richest ever prize, a two-year contract worth £35 million and although even this had been topped, believed to be by McLaren who had the financial might of Marlboro and Mercedes behind them, had opted for Ferrari.

Yet so far off the pace was the famous Prancing Horse that already Schumacher was suggesting that he would not be able to hold on to his title, a suggestion Hill could only laugh at as others pointed out that Ferrari were having winter troubles. Some suggested that Hill must be smiling at Schumacher's troubles. 'I think it's Michael whose laughing,' he said with a smile, alluding to his rival's king's ransom.

McLaren themselves were still struggling to find their old dominant form and that left Benetton, assuming their dominant car of 1995 with the same Renault engine as Williams, could continue to perform with two new drivers. Austrian Gerhard Berger and Frenchman Jean Alesi had been transplanted as a unit from Ferrari to Benetton, an intriguing if not immediately obviously sensible move to take two men who had worked together for so long and knew each other's strengths and weaknesses. Too much comfort zone for them.

Hill's most consistent challenger might be his own team-mate, the very matter-of-fact Villeneuve, 1995 Indycar champion, son of Gilles, second to no man in his own mind, so it would be essential for Hill to produce the real stuff. Not winning the title would therefore be construed as failure and that must mean the end for him in the top line-up.

'I don't think you can approach it with the view that I will not get another go if I do not win it this year,' Hill said. 'That would not be the right way of approaching it. I have got to win it now, I have got to give it my best shot, and you can boil that down to every race, every lap. I have to drive every lap better than the last one.

'The only person who concerns me most is me – I want to get the best out of myself this year. I don't consider the prospect of this being make-or-break. I am concentrating on what I do.

'I don't really want to go into what happened in the past with anyone else, Michael Schumacher or whoever. This is a new season, a time to move on and that is what I intend to do. I know I have a lot of support in the country but I know that there are many who have a different image of me to what you know.

I want people to realise that I have put myself under a lot of pressure. If I look serious or upset at times it is because I feel very passionate about what I do. I have a burning desire to succeed.

'I want to succeed as much for everyone else as for myself. It is not a case of having to reinvent myself. I have not changed one bit. There is a great desire from people in the UK for me to do well and I would not be able to live with myself if I did not do everything possible to give myself the best shot. That includes having the back-up, having the people to look after things off the track. A lot of drivers have their own management companies but that does not rest easily with me because I like to determine my own fate, but I do need support and help and I feel I have that now.

'I felt the need to address other parts of the job, like communicating what I do and what I am about. I enjoy what I do and I want to show that. I want to come across as the real Damon Hill, not as someone false.'

Hill had had the satisfaction of winning the final race of the 1995 season in Adelaide but it was cold comfort for losing the title again and, hardly surprisingly, he was determined not to allow Schumacher any leeway, for the German had won both the on-track battle and the war of words off it. Partly this was a result of Hill hating what he once told me was the bullshit factor of Grand Prix racing, reluctant to get embroiled in the public sniping, the struggle for the better soundbite.

When the pressure had come, Hill had acted normally for most men, applauding Schumacher at the European Grand Prix at Nürburgring in October, talking forlornly of lost hopes and dreams while sitting on the steps of the truck.

Now he had taken advice from professionals. There would be no more sitting on steps, talking while looking up to cameras, psychologically stricken. Now he would adopt a sterner tone rather than his normal quiet, self-effacing manner. While not surrendering the moral high ground, Hill was obviously prepared to adopt a more media-friendly style but one which allowed him to present and retain his personal values of honesty and integrity.

He has a dry sense of humour, running to straight sarcasm

at times, but he has a more rounded view of the world than most drivers and is good company in private. Somehow that fact did not get across as it became obscured by the Schumacher charm offensive.

With every second question concerning Schumacher, not to mention every second headline which linked the two in the melodrama that helped hype F1 to new heights of television audience and newspaper readership, he seemed to be diverted from the task in hand – that of winning the title.

Now he was above it. 'Michael and I were attracted to each other far too often last year,' he said, 'but I have left all that shit behind.

'A lot of what is said is based on gossip and things are simplified to make it easier for people to understand. It does annoy me at times but I have had a winter away, I have my perspective on things and now I am ready for things in a different way.'

Had he changed since 1995, he was asked in the stream of pre-season analysis.

'No,' he insisted, 'not at all. I am the same person, but I have an armour around me which comes from the experiences of 1995. It is always slightly painful to have people point out where you got it wrong, but there is no one more aware of those things than me.

'Conversely, I know where I got it right. It is all about being honest with yourself, committing yourself in the areas you feel you could have been better. 1995 was a difficult year but I learned a lot from the mistakes we made. It has made my own efforts, and the team's efforts, that bit stronger. You have to be honest with yourself before you improve.'

He was looking for more from Williams as a team, and they, for their part, were expecting extra from the man they had taken on as a test driver in 1991 and hired as a driver in 1993 to partner Alain Prost who had then won his fourth title. The little Frenchman promptly retired and Hill, having served his apprenticeship helping set up Nigel Mansell's 1992 world title winning car, was alongside Ayrton Senna until the great

Brazilian's death at San Marino in 1994. He had been forced into the spotlight as number one driver and only just missed out on the title when he tangled with Schumacher in the final race in Australia.

His partner from that year, Scotsman David Coulthard, had moved on to McLaren after eighteen months with Williams who had then opted for the talents of Villeneuve. The team's technical director, Patrick Head, in previewing the season a few weeks earlier from the factory under Didcot's cooling towers in Oxfordshire, was candid in saying: 'It would be fanciful to think Jacques could win the world championship in his first season although I do expect him to win races.

'I think Damon is the man most likely to win this year.'

Head recognised that at times there had been problems technically and in communication in the difficult last few months of the 1995 season.

'There are things we need to do on our side of the team about reliability and pit-stops to sharpen up,' he said. 'We know we have to improve as a team, all of us. Equally, there are things we have told Damon to sort out.'

As an example he highlighted the fact that Hill was stopping two feet short of the mark at refuelling halts, costing valuable seconds as the equipment was moved. He would have to be tidier, tougher, more focused, said Frank Williams whose fellow director, Head, confirmed that Schumacher had interested the team until they heard his salary demands.

'Any team's technical director who had Schumacher would have a rosy glow about getting the best out of the car,' said Head, again not sparing Hill's feelings greatly. As he admitted, he and Williams are not the best 'at giving drivers a cuddle' but tend to let them get on with it after a few down-to-earth pieces of advice, although compliments are also much in evidence.

'The team needed a big bag of gold when Schumacher became available and after we discussed it closely and looked at the bank account, we decided we would not go down that road.'

Williams insisted that his team had the strongest driver line-up but did have words of thought for Hill, saying: 'Overtaking back markers is something Schumacher does very well. When he comes up to them, people acquiesce more than they do for others. Damon needs a different approach and personally, I think he has to give no quarter and pass in a way that says "don't mess with me".

'But he is an extremely fine and accomplished driver and I am sure we will see the best of him this season. It is by no means simply a matter of Williams going out and beating everyone else out of sight. There is great competition and we will all have to work very hard to stay ahead.

'We have disregarded Michael Schumacher's comments about Ferrari not being ready to win the title. This is part of the traditional phoney war. I am sure it will be an outstanding season. Ferrari will win races, McLaren too, and Benetton remain a very good team, brilliant racers.

'This is Damon's fourth year with the team and a lot has been written about his approach. We thought and still think that he is the right man for the job. We believe he will get the job done. Everyone is looking for someone better than Michael Schumacher, each team is searching for this character. Damon has proved that he can beat Michael.'

Hill was already making plans in those directions and he liked what he saw in testing. 'There is a good ambience in the team and they have worked hard on getting their act together, such as in the pit-stops and it is very slick. Everyone is keen to show what they can do. Frank has spoken to me about what we are going to do in 1996. I have spoken to him about ways we can improve the team. Together we are going to get the best out of each other.

'Teamwork and strategy need to be worked on. I need to eradicate as many mistakes as I can. Together we are going to be better prepared, to act on the lessons of '95.

'Formula One is more than ever truly a team sport. Tactics are crucial. It is very important to plan your race but be able to adapt your strategy as the race unfolds. It has become very,

very important to have good guys working with you. I am very much part of a team, because I simply cannot achieve success unless they are right behind me.'

His response to Williams and Head was measured, logical, taking on board their comments and musing over their man-management.

'You get the impression that Patrick would like drivers to be like Alan Jones or Keke Rosberg [Williams's 1980 and 1982 world champions who were hard-driving, pugnacious, forthright men]. He obviously enjoyed the time with them but Williams have had other drivers of different natures and they have all found a way of working at Williams.

'The most important thing is to get the job done, that is what they like.'

The car, the FW18, had been launched on February 9 at the factory with most of the 230 Williams employees there to pay homage to the vehicle of their dreams and their future success. The car was an extension of the FW17B which had lost out in the battle for the constructors' title with Benetton in the previous season but the decision had been taken to use the root of that car and develop it to a higher level.

An improved gearbox, a revised hydraulic installation in an attempt to improve reliability and a new Renault V10 RS08 engine all contributed to a better aerodynamic package, a three-litre money-burning land-based rocket. It felt good. Everything felt good to Hill but that was reflected right across the pits . . . unless you were Ferrari who did seem to be having problems with their car, with it eventually arriving two days before the official test finished.

All the same, Hill was carefully following his new strategy, believing only that which he knew for certain was true, scorning all supposition and rumour.

'You cannot take Schumacher out of the equation for this year,' he insisted. 'They will work very, very hard to catch up and there is no shortage of money to invest.

'He will be a major factor and let's not forget that there are plenty of others. Don't get me wrong. I am not pessimistic.

On the contrary, I am optimistic. That is the mood but I am also realistic enough to know that it is going to be a very hard fight.'

As we headed back from the restaurant we passed the Boca da Inferno, a tiny beach, a gouge in the coastline in which the sea works itself into a frenzy as it battles to find a way back to freedom. A spectacular sight, a scene that perhaps matched the turmoil in Hill's mind at times in the previous season. Certainly not now. It was just beginning but the significance of the two-week break between the Japanese Grand Prix and the Australian Grand Prix which he had won, was now apparent.

Throughout pre-season testing, Williams proved the most complete team with the fastest times and through it all Hill stayed as he had been after dominating in Adelaide, assured, self-confident, anticipating the challenges, not fearing the next onslaught.

After Japan, Head had flown to Australia planning to offer some sorting-out advice to Hill and instead found him in a very upbeat mood and left him to it. That had not changed since, and although no one knew it then, it was not about to for quite some time.

2

A Slick Start

Australian Grand Prix, Melbourne: 10 March

The day Bernie Ecclestone announced that Adelaide was history after eleven years as a Grand Prix venue and that now Melbourne would be the home of the Australian Grand Prix was a bittersweet occasion.

That was almost two years earlier and it sparked disappointment in the Formula One circus, the friendly folks of the city of churches and among many Melbournians who feared for the future of Albert Park, the area designated for the honour of having a Grand Prix run through it. Londoners might also be a mite peeved if someone came along and said they were going to run the British Grand Prix through Hyde Park but the Melbourne city fathers were desperate to enhance Melbourne's already legendary status as a sporting town where people will bet on two flies running up a wall.

Adelaide suited many for it is small and compact, and had welcomed the Grand Prix in an extremely hospitable manner and was easy to get around. There was some flak about the cost of the production to South Australia but most folk in Adelaide reckoned it was an earner which brought publicity and a place in global sport. Melbourne, always in competition with Sydney, could also see the benefits and so the state government of Victoria moved in and captured the prize ... and promptly sparked a wave of protests, parades and petitions from the environmentalists. News that reconstruction work would have to be carried out in Albert Park, described by many as in need of some care and attention, and subsequent reports that 137 trees would have to be axed, provoked downright fury.

11

Such was the venom of the Save Albert Park brigade that work was held up at every stage and when Ecclestone went on an official visit, warning that if people did not want it, there were plenty of other countries waiting for the privilege, he was told that there had been a threat to shoot him.

'He'd better not miss the first time,' said Ecclestone, adding to his reputation as a man who can look after himself.

Those were the circumstances when the F1 circus began arriving in Melbourne, all delighted to exchange the northern winter for the southern hemisphere late summer, and anxious to find out just what four months of rebuilding and testing, innovation and torrents of money, would provide in terms of performance. They came with new hopes and in many cases, new drivers, like football teams in August, all parading their dreams of making the breakthrough or staying on top.

Benetton were still coming to terms with losing the man around whom they had brilliantly built the team, Michael Schumacher, whose skills had brought him back-to-back world championships and contributed hugely to them landing in Australia with the world constructors' title. The idea of a vast amount of Italian lire, or just over £1 million a race for two years, coupled with the magnetic notion that he could attain legendary status by helping the ailing giant that was Ferrari back to the top, was too much to resist.

Out, too, had gone Britain's Johnny Herbert, despite his victories in Britain and Italy, as he and Benetton team principal Flavio Briatore, had hardly exchanged a word in the closing weeks of the 1995 season.

'He couldn't give a damn about me,' said Herbert. 'All they worried about was Michael. That's fine but with all that effort going into one car, it is unfair to compare me unfavourably with Michael as happened.'

Herbert had moved on to the Swiss-based Sauber Ford team who themselves were attempting to come to terms with the news that Jackie Stewart had signed a five-year deal with Ford to run his own Formula One team from 1997. Still, they looked forward to at least one more season of solid Ford backing and decent results from Heinz-Harald Frentzen and Herbert.

Benetton had sent off Schumacher with their best wishes and lured Jean Alesi and Gerhard Berger who had spent three years together at Ferrari.

Famous Sons

The Williams team arrived with Damon Hill entering his fourth season with them and a new partner, Jacques Villeneuve, and the publicity and hype about both men were enormous for a variety of reasons. Their link-up had transcended motorsport media and sporting pages for both were sons of late, great Grand Prix drivers. Damon's father Graham, world champion in 1962 and 1968, had died in a plane crash in 1975. Jacques' dad was Gilles, whose untimely death in 1982 during practice at the Belgian Grand Prix, had helped create a legend of the cavalier of F1, his number 27 Ferrari still revered by the *tifosi*.

Now the sons were working together, not only joined by fate but thrown together as the only real contenders for the world title if the pre-season test times were anything to judge by.

'I am proud to be my father's son but I don't race for him, I race for myself,' insisted Jacques.

Hill was less matter-of-fact about his father but also stressed that he and Villeneuve had not sat around comparing notes on what it was like to be the son of a famous racing driver or how it was that fate had pushed them together.

Villeneuve, 25 years old, Indycar champion, winner of the Indy 500, had not been short of offers to try his hand in Formula One and had made his mind up quickly and fairly easily when Williams arrived in August 1995 offering a test drive at Silverstone. At the back of everyone's mind was the disastrous performance of Michael Andretti in 1993 with McLaren when he got into the car late on circuits he did not know and then opted to commute on Concorde. But Villeneuve had several advantages over Andretti in that he had lived in Monaco with his mother, Joann, and had attended school in Villars in Switzerland. He was much more independent and cosmopolitan and his manager, Craig Pollock, was a Scot with a similar global perspective.

He had done 5000 miles in testing and was refreshingly honest about his objectives, refusing to shelter behind any false mask of undue modesty.

'I want to win the championship,' he said. 'That does not mean I will but I do have a good chance in a Williams car and it is a reason for coming to this team.'

The message to Hill was clear, not aggressively stated, just delivered in his French-Canadian accent in his usual, take-it-or-leave-it style. 'We are going to do our best, but we are not there to help each other. There is no reason not to have a straight fight. There is no way I am going to settle for second.

'Even if you finish second to your team-mate in the championship, after a few years you are not worth anything. It is almost more important to beat your team-mate than anyone else. I have not come here to be number two driver. I would not have done that. If they had told me that I was going to be number two to Damon, I would have said "no way" for I was happy in Indy and I had a good team. There was no point in coming as number two after winning in the States.

'The Williams Renault is a winning car with a winning team and with the marriage we are getting now, there is no excuse and the expectations are fairly high.

'I feel like the team was behind me in testing and that is really important as well when you attack the season. It was important to do the test at Silverstone, not only to see that I could adapt to Formula One or to show that I could, because I felt like I could, but to see how the team works, to see the human side of it – and it was very positive.

'It looked like you could get a great chemistry going on and that is what it needs to win, that is what it takes. This is what we had in the States and to me that is important. If you have got to spend most of the year with the same people, working hard, you need a human relationship. It was difficult to leave the Indy team because we had become good friends but this was a great opportunity and you take opportunities when they are there. We had had great results in the States and the time was right to move, it was not too early.

'It has been important to get mileage in testing. It is important to get into the first race not having to think about the car itself but to feel comfortable in it like an extension of yourself.

'There is so much to learn during the first race weekends, the racing mentality, the other drivers, the tracks.'

The difference between the Indy and F1 cars had been overcome and he declared: 'It is very different in the same level. Basically, it is two very fast, heavy and big cars with small differences but once you get to that level small differences become big because you are not taking big steps in the learning curve any more.

'The F1 car is much lighter, probably about the same down-force so, of course, it is going to brake harder and you are going to go round corners with more speed. So it is more demanding on that side and it takes a little bit of getting used to. The F1 is less stable so everything happens quicker and it will get out of shape quicker but if you have good reflexes you will get it back quicker. There is less time to breathe because everything happens slower on the Indy car.'

His relationship with Hill was 'fine, friendly' he said, but added: 'It is nice if that happens but it is not absolutely necessary to get on with your team-mate. He is the person you most want to beat because you both have the same equipment so that is your easiest guide to how you are driving.

'I won't ask for advice. At this level I don't think anyone asks for advice anyway. How can you translate what you feel in the car to someone else and then that other person translates it back into his own car?

'You have so much feel in driving that you cannot really relate once you are at that level, you cannot really learn much from other people's experiences. You have to experience it yourself so it becomes natural . . . anyway, you are too proud to listen, to take advice.'

He was grateful to have the Villeneuve name, for like Hill it had at least provided a platform to find a few sponsors, but he insisted: 'It does not get you results. When you have a name then you start racing and everybody has got their eyes on you from the first race. In a way, it obliged me to learn quickly and to get used to the pressure, so it actually could have helped on that side as well.'

Ferrari had also been interested in having the name Villeneuve back on a car and there were many who romantically believed it would be perfect to see Jacques in the number 27 red car.

Typically, in his down-to-earth manner, the son cast aside sentiment. 'This is a professional world and I am doing it for myself so that had no importance for my decision,' he said.

'I wanted to be with the best team, with the best possible conditions and with people that you feel there is going to be something with and who will be behind you – and Williams were the most serious in all those discussions.'

All that was left was to re-assert his desire and belief that it was not impossible for him to win the world title and to issue a small warning to those who might see him as the rich little rookie.

'Once you know who is dirty and who is not, then you can pay them back on the race track if necessary but there is no point in fighting with words before the season starts – that is just a waste of energy.'

Hill, who had had a few run-ins with his 1995 partner, David Coulthard, knew exactly from the start just what Villeneuve was about but was unfazed, unaffected, perfectly happy.

'We get on fine as Jacques says and I would expect him to be challenging me all the way in the Williams team,' said Hill. 'I don't have any problems and I don't foresee any. I have had a really good winter and have worked closely with the Williams team and now I cannot wait for the season to start.

'I have learned a lot in my three seasons and I aim to use all that experience this year. After two years as runner-up there is only one way to go and that is up.'

New Season Hopes

Coulthard had replaced Mark Blundell, who had moved to Indycar, at McLaren Mercedes, insisting it was a good move as he teamed up with Finland's Mika Hakkinen, who had defied the pessimists by returning to Australia to drive despite spending sixteen hours in a coma after crashing in Adelaide in the final race of the previous season.

An emergency tracheotomy had been performed in the car, he had needed operations on both ears, one side of his face had been slightly affected by nerve damage and he had lost 22 lbs while lying in hospital for weeks but a hard winter of physiotherapy and fitness training had brought Hakkinen back although it was only at a recent test that he had declared himself fully fit.

He had described the feeling at the test in the South of France in February, saying it had gone quiet among the mechanics when he put on his helmet and sat in the McLaren car for the first time since the accident. 'Normally it is noisy but everyone was a bit nervous. When I accelerated, it felt fantastic. I thought "this is great, this is fun" and I did not feel scared any more.'

It was a timely reminder of the price the sport can extort from the drivers and one which was to be reinforced in the race by the new-look, freshly sponsored Benson & Hedges Jordan Peugeot team who arrived in gold colours, with high hopes and a good bank balance with Eddie Jordan declaring, 'We want to be the fourth best team this season, maybe ahead of McLaren. It is time we won a race.'

He had recruited veteran Brit, Martin Brundle, who had turned them down two years earlier, to replace Ulsterman Eddie Irvine, sold to Ferrari in a surprise deal when they were looking for a partner for Schumacher.

The new season had brought several other changes. Qualifying was now reduced to one Saturday session instead of being split over two days. Friday was now free practice, the theory being that as at Silverstone in 1995, the drivers would not be able to sit in the garages on a wet day because they knew they could not improve on their times from the previous day.

Teams had two one-hour sessions on Fridays to find a set-up, experiment with different aerodynamic settings or fuel loads to see how the cars were working. The main difference in the cars was the higher cockpit sides, ordered by the sport's governing body, the FIA, to give more protection to drivers from side-swipe accidents.

Already there was controversy for Jordan's interpretation of the rule had upset Benetton who claimed that the measurement had been taken from a different point and the sides were not as high and therefore less of an aerodynamic drag.

Gerhard Berger, the most experienced driver, opened proceedings in Melbourne by saying that it was more that Hill had lost the title in 1995, less that Schumacher had won. 'He had an advantage and lost it,' said the Austrian, 'but now it is a new year, different things, and Hill will not be in the same situation again. He lost his concentration last year but I think he is very good and he will have learned from that. He is the favourite to win the championship but we will make life hard for him.'

Martin Brundle, looking at the prospects for the season, thought Hill and the Williams would blow everyone away but was worried that Hill had lost the previous championship because of 'clumsy manoeuvres' against Schumacher at Silverstone and Monza when they both ended up in the kitty litter.

'The bottom line,' he said, 'is that he is not as gifted as Schumacher . . . but no one is.'

Hill had arrived via Bondi beach, meeting up with former world 500 cc motorbike champion Barry Sheene, who lives and works as a television commentator in Australia.

'I did the tourist thing, the beach, jet-skiing, played some golf, looked around Sydney. It was great, got me in the Australian mood,' said a jaunty Hill when he flew into Melbourne.

The protests to save the park rolled on with demonstrators having slashed marquees a few days earlier and scattered feathers on the circuit although someone presumably forgot the tar. They were still seeking injunctions, threatening to scatter broken glass around and one man had suggested he would throw himself in front of a racing car.

Forty years earlier, Stirling Moss had won on the circuit which was now a 3.27 mile combination of fast and slow corners in a scenic setting around a lake with the high-rise elegance of Melbourne in the background.

Hill had seen the protestors as he arrived at the track where frantic final preparations were still being made and he was diplomatic. 'They are concerned about the environment and so am I,' he said. 'We should not appear to be oblivious to their concerns.

'I like the circuit, I went round it for the first time in a hire car and it is a long track which looks like a mixture of Adelaide and Canada. It has a nice straight, good quick corners, plenty of overtaking areas and is quite fast. I am quite confident about my chances but don't let us forget about Ferrari. They have their problems but they will get it right.

'I don't know if that will be here but Michael is a very competitive person. We did have a physical attraction to each other last year but it would be great if we could steer clear of each other. We do speak. I spoke to him in testing.'

Did he wish him well, he was asked.

'I wish everyone well,' said Hill. 'Love does not enter into it in F1 – respect is the thing.

'We all want to compete. I think it would be great to come away from the first race of the season with a serious helping of points. We have a little bit of an edge right now but the pressure is never-ending.

'Jacques is in the same competitive car so there is always the danger of being beaten. I am being held up as favourite for the title and rightly so. I don't see a change in driving style or feel that is necessary. You have to be aggressive, that is the nature of motor-racing. Aggression on its own will not be enough, skill comes into it, too.'

Perhaps there was a touch of foresight in Hill when he added: 'If it comes down to Jacques and myself going for the world championship, then at least the win will go to Williams.'

Around the same time, Renault Sport president Patrick Faure was saying that he could see no reason why, if they continued to win, his company would pull out of Formula One, a comment later to haunt him.

Schumacher had gone off for the day. There were dolphins swimming in the bay but already it seemed that the sharks were out to get him but he was as sunny as the weather despite a reliability-challenged testing programme.

Problems with the gearbox, handling difficulties, talk of a new nose for the car were all discussed in the pits but Schumacher insisted he was not downhearted although he did have the warmth of a £35 million contract to soothe the pain.

'I chose Ferrari because it has a history and I want to be part of that. There was a bigger offer but I wished to go to Ferrari. It was not just about money, that is not my motivation. I don't care what other people think of me, the only expectations that matter are the ones I have set myself.

'The situation here is not rose-tinted but after three to four races we will be competitive.'

Hot Start

When the engines fired up for the first time on the morning of Thursday March 7 for the familiarisation practices allowed for a new circuit, excitement was high in Melbourne and sure enough, car number one, the Ferrari F310, driven by the champion, Michael Schumacher, was out first.

Computer simulations forecast a lap time of 1 minute 33.450 seconds but it was Martin Brundle who set the season's first flying lap, 1 minute 42.416 seconds in his Jordan. Maybe this was the start of something big for Martin . . . little did anyone know what a dramatic race was in store for him.

Hill was next out, drove round to get a feel of the place for one lap and returned the spare car to the garage to move out in his racing machine. The financially challenged Forti team provided the first little drama of the season when some rubber in the engine bay caught fire briefly and soon after Hill got serious with a lap which was one and a half seconds quicker than anyone else.

Pedro Lamy in the Minardi had the distinction of the first skid off the circuit and the session ended six minutes early when Luca Badoer abandoned his spun and stalled Forti on a turn, forcing a red flag.

By that time Hill, the fastest in the session, had done 14 laps to Villeneuve's 15 and the words 'encouraging' and 'reasonable' popped up like rabbits from drivers and teams. Villeneuve got the better of Hill in the second session but as an early indicator of the season, Schumacher was struggling down in ninth.

'It is a fun track,' declared Hill. 'Jacques really got on with the job and there is going to be some tough competition between us. Everyone has always said he is very quick, the car is working well so it is a good sign for us because the car is capable of doing it.'

On Friday, the work continued and Villeneuve was first in to the 1 minute 32s, more than half a second faster than anyone else had managed. Schumacher was closing in after locking up and doing minor damage as he careered through the gravel trap.

Hill's response came later when he went quickest on 1.32.159 and followed that with the second fastest time of the day. It was looking good and Hill admitted: 'The pace is hotting up now . . . we are just experimenting with set-ups and dialling in the car . . . it is a little difficult to know what everyone else is up to.'

Jos Verstappen earned the first fine of the season, $2500, after the Dutchman abandoned his car on the circuit after a spin and removed his steering wheel to take back to the garage.

The official weigh-in for the start of the season, a controversial issue twelve months earlier when Schumacher weighed in heavy, was a calmer affair but this time Rubens Barrichello was the scales-crusher at 79 kilos with Hill fourth heaviest at

75.5 kilos (11 st 8 lbs) and little Andrea Montermini just 65 kilos.

Whatever the weight difference, Villeneuve made light of every obstacle; the rookie on the new circuit in a new car stunned everyone with a lap seven minutes from the end of the qualifying session on another hot day by ripping round in 1 minute 32.371 seconds. That edged out Hill by a mere 0.138 of a second. The day belonged to the new men for Schumacher also found himself squeezed out by his team-mate, Irvine, who cheered the Ferrari fans by taking third on the grid, but still a fraction over half a second behind Villeneuve.

Villeneuve had now become the first debutant to claim pole since Carlos Reutemann in 1972, but again he was calm about the whole thing, saying: 'I am very satisfied so far but I still have a lot to learn in the race – and I am sure I will learn tomorrow if we get to turn one after the start. There was no special tactic today. I just went as fast as I could.'

Pretty simple, really.

Hill was impressed. 'He is quick and he has obviously learned the track as fast as anyone. I never expected it to be easy. It motivates me and I am quite happy about that. We are looking strong as a team.'

Schumacher had again been bedevilled by gearbox trouble, this time the casing had cracked, and he had to use the spare car and that left him saying: 'Let's not dream' about his chances of winning the race. Ferrari had airfreighted new parts from Italy overnight but they were already struggling to keep up with the pace of problems.

The two Fortis had travelled a 24,000 mile round trip to miss out on the action because they were outside the 107 per cent margin of Villeneuve's time.

Miracle Escape

Villeneuve sat quietly in the car proudly on pole position on Sunday afternoon, only the third driver in Formula One history to start his first race in such a position, the other two being

Carlos Reutemann and Mario Andretti. Hill sheltered from the heat under an umbrella. The two Ferraris sat immediately behind the Williams cars and on row three sat two of the fastest starters in the sport, Hakkinen and Alesi.

Ahead lay 58 laps, 189.89 miles, round the park as the temperature hovered in the early 90s. A new sequenced starting light system replaced the line 'when the lights turned to green' for now it was a countdown to five sets of red lights which are activated for one second, extinguished and off everyone goes . . . hopefully.

When the new procedure had done its job, Villeneueve held pole as he powered away but Hill was having trouble getting the car off the start line, a botched job he was to describe later as 'making a pig's ear of it'. As he struggled, both Ferraris rocketed past and already Hill looked like having a long, hot race – but his luck was about to change.

Brundle, starting at the back after a technical problem, had accelerated hard but in the tangle near the rear, Coulthard found himself pushed across by a Ligier, the Jordan car clipped him and launched itself off the rear wheel into the air at 180 mph.

It rolled upside down and flew over the top of Johnny Herbert's Sauber before hitting the ground ahead, careering along the concrete and splitting in two as he ploughed into the first gravel trap on the left at the end of the straight.

The crowd's screams turned to exultant, relieved cheers as Brundle, his helmet scraped, suddenly emerged from underneath the wreckage. He had a quick look at the destruction, saw the race had been red-flagged and set off to the pits at a run. A hurried discussion and then he was off running again, this time in search of the F1 doctor, Professor Sid Watkins, to ask if he could drive in the re-started race.

'He said he had passed the first medical check and would like to drive as he felt fine. I asked him what month it was, he knew and off he went running again,' said Watkins.

Brundle was equally cool about the whole thing, later saying: 'I can remember everything about it. When I went up in the air I thought "Martin, this is not good" because when you are flying you are totally out of control. I pulled my head in as far as it would go. When the car came to a rest I thought I was not going to get out and I could feel something dripping on me. I thought it was fuel but it was fluid from my bottle.'

Herbert described it as 'like a scene from *Top Gun* where he flies upside down and I could actually see Martin in the cockpit.'

At the re-start, Brundle was there in the spare car and this time Hill powered the Williams away into second place. Schumacher clung on, forcing his Ferrari past Irvine who gave ground, saying it was not diplomatic but smart as the German was faster. It was valiant of the world champion but it came as no surprise to anyone when, after a pit-stop, he was forced out on the 33rd lap with brake problems.

Irvine had already met up and survived a wheel-to-wheel clash with his predecessor at Ferrari, Jean Alesi, when the hot-blooded Frenchman attempted to take fourth on the tenth lap. It ended in tears for the Benetton man who limped back to the pits and out of the race.

Villeneuve thundered on, held his lead through the pit-stops and looked set for victory. The only sign of trouble was the changing colour of Hill's car which appeared to be turning a horrible shade of yellow. Suddenly, five laps from the end, the reason for the re-spray became obvious as Villeneuve began to slow after fighting fiercely to hold off Hill, even getting sideways through the chicane at one point.

Computer readouts in the Williams garage had indicated for some time that Villeneuve had been losing oil and that was spraying all over Hill who had radioed to the pits to let them know. Now it was obvious that there would not be enough oil left for Villeneuve to finish the race at his speed and he was ordered to slow down. He queried the situation but after discussion, it was clear that it was either ease off or suffer a blown engine. Hill powered past and finished the race looking like an old-style racer, oily and sweaty but with a huge smile.

He had the win he so craved and, in doing so, equalled the fourteen career wins of his father, Graham.

'I can't describe what it feels like,' said Hill. 'It is a long time since I was leading the world championship and I do feel on top of the world. Everyone in the team deserves this result, it was terrific.

'I had a great race with Jacques and I have started the season where I finished off the last one.

'I don't think there is going to be anything given away between the two of us this season. Jacques has shown he is a racer. The crowd must have enjoyed that. It was a thriller.'

Understandably, Villeneuve was less overjoyed, saying: 'I was very happy until five laps from the end. It is disappointing to lead most of the race and then have to slow down, but the race was fun and it was a great battle with Damon.

'When I heard the team screaming on the radio for two laps I understood there was something wrong and then the red lights started coming on and I knew the oil was going down. It is annoying that you have to slow down that way to end up second but second for the first race is great and I am very happy about that.'

Renault technical director Bernard Dudot confirmed the oil pressure problem, saying: 'We had confirmation of Jacques' talent. He also showed he is very mature because obviously he had a problem in the last 15 laps, and when we asked him to reduce speed he perfectly understood it was the only solution for the team to have a 1–2 finish.'

The Williams team was delighted, sad for Villeneuve, pleased for Hill, happy with their own performance and Head, the technical director, could not hide his pleasure as he said: 'Jacques did superbly well but we should not be surprised. He is a racer and has had very good results before.

'There was nothing we could do about his situation but he accepted it and we got a 1–2 finish which is wonderful for the team and Renault. We are certainly not in a position to be tactical and tell one of the drivers to slow down or "you win this race, you win the next". It is not in their contracts.

'We all know in the team and everyone will be told that our two guys are racing each other. We have been in that situation before and we got it wrong in 1986 with Nigel Mansell and

Nelson Piquet. That is a long way off but if we get to that situation, we will have to look at it again.'

Even in victory, Hill found himself under pressure, with some saying that despite his experience, he had been shown up by a new boy who would have won except for the technical problem, but he was assured and defiant, pointing out that he had been applying big pressure from a perfect attacking position before Villeneuve was slowed.

'I am happy, I was never outpaced and I feel more confident about my driving than before,' Hill said. 'I don't care what the so-called experts say. I am very pleased and I know that Jacques is too. We are going to have some tough battles this season and not just between ourselves. But I am very happy to be leaving Australia with 10 points. It is a great start.'

His view appeared to be confirmed by Head. 'I think Damon was driving well within himself. It looked that way on our read-outs. It would certainly have been an interesting last few laps. I don't have a file on how Jacques responds under pressure but Damon was certainly right on it and seemed to have more in reserve.'

The battlelines had been drawn. Villeneuve had thrown down the gauntlet and a few gallons of oil which Hill had survived. Schumacher was struggling, Benetton promised more but Hill flew home with his father's memory fresh but keeping everything in perspective by saying: 'My dad won fourteen races but he also won two world titles.

'I am not even thinking about being up there with him. I am proud to have won as many Grands Prix but there is no question of thinking about being better or anything like that. It is a different era and my aim is to win this year's championship. That is all I am thinking about.'

In the 46-year history of F1 racing, the winner of the first race on 21 occasions had gone on to win the world title and for the previous six seasons, that trend had followed unbroken for Ayrton Senna, Mansell, Alain Prost and Schumacher.

Hill did not even pause to contemplate this. He would not

allow the Fates to determine his future. That would be determined by his own hand.

Race 1: Australian Grand Prix

Result	Drivers (overall)	Constructors (overall)
1. Damon Hill (GB)	1. Hill 10	1. Williams 16
2. Jacques Villeneuve (Can)	2. Villeneuve 6	2. Ferrari 4
3. Eddie Irvine (GB)	3. Irvine 4	3. Benetton 3
4. Gerhard Berger (Aut)		
5. Mika Hakkinen (Fin)		
6. Mika Salo (Fin)		

3

Rainman

Brazilian Grand Prix, Interlagos: 31 March

Very little is perfect in Brazil except some of the women and a few footballers but as he drove in from the airport to downtown São Paulo, one of the less scenic but more interesting drives in Grand Prix racing, Damon Hill's mind was on a perfect weekend.

He wanted the lot and nothing would stand in his way. In a country where most of the population live on dreams and little else, it seemed not out of place. Why should Hill not go for the full house from pole to victory? It seemed fanciful, but no worse than some of the early season stories which were flying around F1 as the teams decanted in South America.

Patrick Head was busy denying yet another leaked version of the official report into Ayrton Senna's death in 1994 which again had come to the conclusion that steering failure was the cause of the crash at the San Marino Grand Prix.

McLaren boss Ron Dennis was denying rumours that four times world champion, Alain Prost, the team's technical adviser, was preparing a takeover bid as team owner. Tom Walkinshaw, the tough Scot who had masterminded Benetton's rise and rise as technical director before moving to Ligier after Benetton principal Flavio Briatore bought the team, was in the market, however. He had moved in to take over the Arrows team, which had become Footwork for part of their existence, and was preparing to move teams.

ITV were denying that their takeover of Grand Prix racing from 1997 would mean advertisements every two minutes and loss of continuity in events and Ferrari were not denying that

29

they would resort to using 1995's gearbox, suspension and diffuser as they struggled to overcome handling problems.

No one was denying that the traffic in São Paulo would be as desperate as usual or that the best moment of the week would be the departure to Argentina after the race. Michael Schumacher was encouraged by testing work since Australia but his noises off seemed to have more to do with giving team morale a boost before Brazil. The Autodromo José Carlos Race Circuit, to give the 2.684 mile long track its full moniker, was reshaped for the return of Grand Prix racing from Rio in 1990, a comeback which may have more than a little to do with the city being Ayrton Senna's home. Now it was a pilgrimage to his grave in a cemetery not too far from the Interlagos district where *favellos*, the shanty house areas made from cardboard, pieces of metal, wood, anything that provided shelter, were used even though there are some extremely comfortable houses across the main road from the circuit.

The city is a smog-bound, traffic-snarled sprawling mess where the two extremes are millionaires' villas with staffs and swimming pools and shacks where people wash in puddles. There seems to be little middle ground but there is a vibrant, not to say desperate air, in the conurbation. A haze hangs over the high-rise buildings, military police are everywhere and stray children and dogs fill the streets . . . as Schumacher was to discover.

The Williams team, constantly living under the cloud of the Senna investigation, were given a boost when his family chose the time to announce that they would not be suing the Oxfordshire-based racing team over the accident. Senna's sister Vivian confirmed that they were not considering legal action, saying: 'Frank Williams is a member of the Senna Foundation and the family has a lot of respect for him. We do not think he would be negligent.'

True Form

Damon Hill arrived feeling good, declaring that he would like the full set this weekend – pole position, fastest lap, victory. 'That is the perfect race. There is no disputing that, no one can argue with that,' he said, referring indirectly to continued sniping that he had only won in Melbourne because of his team-mate's technical fault.

Yet at the end of the first day's practice, it was Benetton who had captured the limelight, making amends for a poor performance in Australia with Jean Alesi first and Gerhard Berger second. Neither of the Williams drivers looked too nonplussed by their showings, Hill fifth, Villeneuve down among the plodders in fifteenth. As they pointed out, however, Friday had become a day of experimentation now that it had lost its qualifying status.

Those who watched carefully saw that Hill was rightfully in confident mood for he had gone through both parts of the session on a single set of tyres and had even lost running time when a water pipe came loose early in the session. He threw in a spin for good measure and emerged to say: 'We know where we are. I think we are competitive.'

Villeneuve, too, was less than despondent about his low placing, also using only one set of tyres and working hard to learn the tricky circuit.

Alesi had worked with a heavy fuel load to test his car but he and Berger had used new sets of tyres during testing which can be worth 1.5 seconds a lap, and they lacked the speed of the Williams.

Barrichello put in a couple of quick laps to please the locals who had turned out to watch the local hero, but eventually a Peugeot engine failure forced him down to tenth place. Schumacher had little to cheer, working hard for seventh but Eddie Irvine crashed badly on his first out lap in the morning session. He emerged unscathed but the car was a 24-hour rebuild.

Villeneuve was complaining of media hype, constant prying,

but this was due to his decision to stay at the beach home of Senna, at Angra dos Reis, flying into the circuit each day on a Senna Foundation helicopter. The link was too much for the Brazilian supporters who were keen to shift some of their dreams to the Williams driver.

The crowds at Interlagos proclaimed their new love on banners and in cheers but it seemed to have backfired for Villeneuve who said: 'It was supposed to be a quiet few days but everyone seeemed to find out I was there and I could not go out of the door without photographers being there. That was annoying, it was not what I wanted.'

All week, Villeneuve had outpaced the rest of the grid in the media, his face appearing on television, newspapers and magazines. There was a fashion shoot, MTV appearance, interviews and Barrichello must have felt like the forgotten man in his own town.

Villeneuve was careful not to extend the Senna link himself, playing it down although he had now done a deal on marketing with Senna's former manager, Julian Jakobi, and said simply: 'I never met him, that is a pity. He was a great driver'.

Still the talk was of Villeneuve's opening drive in Australia with Prost saying the world title would be between the Williams men, declining to say who he would tip, and finding support from Jackie Stewart who described Villeneuve's debut drive as 'the best I have seen from any driver'.

Villeneuve was quizzed on his feelings towards Hill but insisted: 'Why should our relationship suffer because we are competing with each other? You can be the best of friends and still have a go at each other on the track. As long as there's respect and you don't put the other guy in the wall, then it is fine. I like being on the edge and fighting.'

Heinz-Harald Frentzen made a $10,000 contribution to FIA funds for passing the chequered flag twice after free practice ended but it was Hill who was set to make his critics pay. In qualifying, Hill showed his true form. He had held much in hand and on a brilliant sunny Saturday, he blitzed the opposition.

Barrichello had sent the locals into a noisy frenzy with a very quick lap which put him on top, lapping in 1 minute 19.092 seconds. At last the driver and Jordan had made the breakthrough but then Hill nosed out of the garage, wound up the car in the heat and to the astonishment of everyone in the pits came in almost a second faster, 0.981 to be exact.

Villeneuve had tried but just a touch too hard and his car was damaged when it ran wide off one of the track's big bumps and damaged the rear suspension. He returned late to put in a third place time, 1.1 behind Hill but Schumacher was pleased to be fourth, even if he was 1.3 seconds off the pace.

Hill had forecast that Ferrari would be more on the pace in Brazil and Patrick Head, Williams's technical director, had also been impressed by the Italian team's improvement and hard work in Melbourne.

As usual, Irvine's cold view of reality had proved correct for he had said: 'Close the gap by Brazil? I hope they are right but I would be surprised. Some major things need to be sorted out first. We have a long way to go to beat Williams.'

Stormy Weather

So it proved, but Sunday dawned threatening rain, an equaliser for the other teams who saw a chance to take on Williams. The morning warm-up was very hot, muggy, and uneventful but as the race approached, so did the dark, grey storm clouds.

Hill had a sense of foreboding as he watched the skies explode with rain, thunder and lightning. Yet the roll of thunder was the sound of doom for his rivals who had hoped to capitalise on wet weather. Hill had been startled by a bolt of lightning he saw strike the ground not far from the car as he drove round the parade lap but he was not alarmed enough to put him off when the start came.

The 35-year-old Londoner disappeared into a curtain of rain, leaving the men behind driving blind in plumes of spray. Even Alesi, the most daring of drivers in the rain, admitted afterwards: 'It was impossible to see anything. I was a little bit scared. I had to fight with a big nerve. It was not very nice and it was not nice being lapped by Hill.'

Rarely do F1 drivers admit as much and Alesi's statement did nothing to compromise the bravery of those who took part in the 71-lap blast over 190 miles. He undoubtedly spoke for the entire field. Alesi had battled through to second place, 20 seconds behind Hill who utilised his place in the sun off pole with all the skill and opportunity it afforded him to take his second victory of the season.

As the others drove through the wall of water, Hill drove on relentlessly with a reasonably clear view of his immediate future to establish an impregnable lead.

'I took advantage of a clear circuit and capitalised on that,' said Hill who held off Barrichello's brave bid for first place until the first corner. By the fourth lap, Hill had moved to an 11.5 second lead. Not only did Hill win but he also had the satisfaction of overtaking Schumacher for the first time in a race and surpassed his father Graham's career total of fourteen victories.

Hill had met the man regarded as the world's greatest footballer, Pele, before the start but Pele could only marvel at the men who then went out to drive in the name of sport on a 2.6 mile black river that was Interlagos. Only half an hour before the race began, the crowds were sweltering in a 92 degree heat, teams were concerned about driver fatigue and tyre blistering was a worry in a heat-haze on the south side of the city. But it was more bow-waves than Mexican waves as they powered round.

The rain eased and now a dry line began to appear. Alesi powered after Hill and it was clear both were on one-stop strategies. Alesi was pulling the Englishman who was driving with due care and attention but the fiery Frenchman ran wide as he pushed on, lost time and a place as Barrichello slipped past.

Just as Hill was preparing to make his stop on lap 40, the rain came on again. Would he go for slicks or wets? Slicks it was, a gamble, but it paid off and after that the race was over. Alesi moved into the lead until his stop when Hill moved back to the lead.

Nine laps from the end, Formula One fans braced themselves for another deadly duel as Hill came round behind Schumacher but the German gave way gracefully. 'It was an unusual experience to go past Michael with both of us staying apart and not going off the track,' said Hill with a big smile.

Villeneuve moved up to second place but the French-Canadian found himself under real pressure in the wet from Alesi who took the line on the 26th lap, forcing the Williams car wide. Villeneuve lost it, spun into the gravel and as he walked back in the rain, Hill swept past, 17 seconds in the lead.

'I made a mistake,' admitted Villeneuve candidly.

The casualty rate increased. Gerhard Berger abandoned his Benetton in disgust in the garage and Scotland's David Coulthard completed a miserable weekend when his gallant efforts to move from fourteenth on the grid to ninth ended when a mechanical problem saw him slide off.

All around they were sliding and spinning but Hill drove imperiously to take the fifteenth win of his career, a marked contrast to his previous Brazilian race where he led from the start until his car broke down, a blow which damaged him deeper than it should have.

Pele was waiting at the end to give Hill his trophy. 'I really did have a sense of foreboding at the start,' said Hill. 'Lightning hit the ground not far from the car and I just concentrated on getting a good start. I knew it would be difficult for the guys behind and being out in front was not easy but easier.

'The conditions were, shall we say, risky. Obviously I was in the best position but even so there were rivers on the track and quite heavy rainfall even after the start. I can hardly imagine what it was like for the guys behind. I was just eager to use that gap. I had to make hay while the rain came down!'

Schumacher confirmed the view of danger. 'The rain actually started coming down again while we were sitting in the cars waiting to go out,' said the world champion. 'There could be no discusssion about not racing but I told my team to ask the race director to be very careful in those conditions because it was undrivable and we could not have raced.

'I could see nothing. I was just trying to keep the car on the road.'

Hill now had the start he dreamed of before the season: a commanding lead of fourteen points over Villeneuve; his fiercest rival, Schumacher, with only four points; and the Benettons showing little sign of the performance level of the previous year when they were constructors' champions.

· Now he was more willing to address the psychological landmark of surpassing his father in wins but he was careful not to appear superior except in numerical terms.

'I am very proud to have won fifteen races,' he said. 'I don't want to take anything away from my father's achievement at all. I do think I am a little bit more out there on my own – I am more Damon Hill than the son of Graham now.'

It was as close as he would get to allowing others to glimpse a release from the pigeonhole of being the offspring of a man who became a legend in his own lifetime, a real-life adventurer, instantly recognisable with a smooth style and a handy line in witty repartee.

Almost immediately, Hill played it all down, insisting: 'Too much has been made of it, to be honest. My focus is so much on getting the best results for the team and on my performance this season that all other things are asides and they come with success.

'I have won three Grands Prix on the trot, Adelaide, Melbourne and São Paulo, and that is an achievement for me. 'Now I am fifth in the all-time British lists behind Mansell, Stewart, Clark and Moss and that feels great.

'I am an enormous admirer of great racing drivers. Nelson Piquet turned up here and I go "wow, it's Nelson Piquet". I have followed the sport for long enough and viewed it from afar and I am impressed by the greats. It still thrills me a little bit and I find it odd to associate myself up there. Statistics are one of the things drivers are judged on and my winning average is going up again. It is one of the best ever.

'My attitude is to keep pressing on and get the best results I can while we have an advantage. The competition will get tougher and it will be more difficult as we go on.

'We have been through it last year. I was leading the championship by Imola and then lost a lot of points. Then I pulled back Michael's lead to ten points by Hungary. He had had a big lead. The pressure will be on all the way through fourteen more races – the bulk of the championship is yet to come.'

This was Hill on a high, loving and living the moments of success after so many moments of despair. There were no critics this time for he had won a tough race with undoubted ability and he was revelling in the conversation before leaving the circuit.

'I feel great,' he confirmed. 'I am enjoying it all the time. It is nice when you have a great car to drive. It is a case of feeling confident. If I get a chance to rub it in, I will.

'I had a wry smile on my face as I passed Schumacher. I don't want to gloat. Michael has his job to do at Ferrari. He is a great asset to them and he will bring them on – they have taken a step back with the old gearbox this weekend but they will be back.'

Yet, like those sitting with him, he recognised that a psychological barrier had been removed by his overtaking of Schumacher.

'It is a relief to have beaten Michael,' said Hill, nodding in agreement with his own words. 'I enjoyed every duel we had I would not give that up for anything. I enjoyed every time I had a close race with Michael.'

If it sounded like a mantra, a course in positivism, it seemed to be working, but as Hill admitted almost immediately, he would not object to racing out front in future.

'I would have no complaints about racing against myself. Let's not get too carried away, though. Only two races have gone and a lot changes in this sport very quickly.

'The car is good and I want to capitalise on that while we

are in the lead. Benetton and Ferrari will be tough and Jordan are obviously doing a very good job. Enjoy it while you can is what I say. I don't feel I cannot be beaten but I do feel very confident in myself.

'I am as much in competition with myself as with anyone else. I want to get the best out of myself. I want to eke out as much performance from myself as I can and to drive myself to the limit of my capabilities because I think I am quite a good driver.'

His bosses felt the same. Frank Williams declared: 'I think Damon did a very good job. The conditions made it very difficult. I can never be convinced that the car is perfect – but even if it is, it still has to be driven perfectly to win.'

And Patrick Head also opined: 'It was a fine drive by Damon. There were plenty of opportunities out there to make mistakes but he did not make any. He just pulled away brilliantly in the first part of the race and gave himself the opportunity to control things from there on.

'We cannot afford to be complacent. After three or four races last year everyone was saying we were on for it but then we started to lose it a bit. This time forewarned is forearmed. We will be working and working to keep our advantage but it will not be easy.'

The only wrong move Hill made came now when he and his wife Georgie drove three hours down the coast to a holiday hotel – only to find it was busy and full of people who wanted his autograph while all he wanted was some peace and quiet. He turned around and headed back and on up to Rio. Even that could not spoil his mood for long and as he headed out to São Paulo airport he could reflect on making his dream come true.

'Pole, fastest lap, a win – the perfect weekend,' he said, recalling his forecast on arrival. 'That is another nice statistic to have. Now to win in Argentina and leave South America with full points.'

Race 2: Brazilian Grand Prix

Result	Drivers (overall)	Constructors (overall)
1. Damon Hill (GB)	1. Hill 20	1. Williams 26
2. Jean Alesi (Fra)	2=Villeneuve 6	2. Benetton 9
3. Michael Schumacher (Ger)	2=Alesi 6	3. Ferrari 8
4. Mika Hakkinen (Fin)		
5. Mika Salo (Fin)		
6. Olivier Panis (Fra)		

4

Hill's Hat-Trick

I f Damon Hill was purring when he swept into the broad *avenidas* of Buenos Aires, Michael Schumacher had found that these dog days of a lucrative but frustrating season had become literal. Here was another turn around in fortunes and styles. Hill had switched from his holiday by the sea with his wife and had gone to Rio de Janeiro with Georgie and had stayed at the same hotel as his physiotherapist, Austrian Erwin Gollner. Five days on the famous beaches were enjoyable but he also spent much of it under Gollner's guidance, running, exercising, working in the hotel gym, combining work and play, sight-seeing and socialising. It was also almost certainly where he picked up a stomach bug which troubled him all through the Argentinian campaign. His overall fitness helped him through four days when he spent as much time running to the toilet as he did running on the track.

Schumacher had different things to consider for his wife, Corinna, had adopted a dog, or rather it adopted her, when it followed the lovely lady across the car park early in the build-up to the Brazilian Grand Prix.

A small, tan, smooth-coated, prick-eared mongrel which looked as if it had been delivered by Disney central casting, the dog suddenly realised there was a different life to sniffing round the rubbish tips of some of the Interlagos shanty districts, battling for survival with hundreds of other strays.

Within a day it had become something of a celebrity and by Saturday it was being examined from the tip of its nose to the end of its bushy tail by a veterinary surgeon who probed it,

41

X-rayed it and passed it fit after submitting the kind of bill that only the world champion could deal with.

Despite a valiant last minute bid by another enterprising local, who saw the dog on television and declared that this was his long-lost friend for life, Flea, as the mutt had been aptly named, flew with the Schumachers to Argentina.

When that was over, the millionaire mutt, already looking chubbier on the best that Ferrari and five-star hotel chefs could produce, was on his way first-class courtesy of Lufthansa to Frankfurt. A couple more tests and he moved to Monaco to the luxury flat but now has shifted to Switzerland where the Schumachers have bought a mansion. It was a romantic story which even Disney could not have dreamed up and certainly happier than Michael's season was turning out to be.

Any ideas of another fairytale coming true were firmly rejected by four times world champion Alain Prost and McLaren boss Ron Dennis who both quashed rumours that the little Frenchman was about to return to the cockpit. Prost had applied for and been given a superlicence required by all drivers but it was stressed that he was simply covering for test driver Jan Magnussen, who was on International Touring Car business, and Prost would remain as an adviser to the team.

McLaren and Mercedes did not deny, however, that they had been the victims of industrial espionage, for early in the week an intruder had entered the garage at the track during the night and removed an air filter and airbox to examine the engine. Dennis had no doubts that the engine spy knew exactly what he was looking for.

A Bumpy Ride

Schumacher arrived still smarting from being overtaken by Hill in Brazil, saying: 'It was not very nice and you can say that.' He was having a rough ride but the circuit at Buenos Aires, which once boasted a superb, exciting track, is now an emasculated, tight, 2.64 mile, ten-cornered affair. A year earlier the drivers had complained bitterly about how bumpy it was and asked for resurfacing to be carried out.

Some had been but two big bumps, which acted as launch pads for the cars remained, and when the cars raced in Friday's free practice session, Schumacher was the most spectacular of all, battling with the machine as it fought to go its own way in collusion with a track which encouraged waywardness.

But it was Hill who led the field and the protests after being forced to worry about his dental crowns rather than the championship version. He could move into the all-time top ten winners list if he won this race but he was more concerned over movement in the car after two jarring sessions and, for once, he found an ally in Schumacher.

'There is a bump on the back straight and I am worried about the crowns in my teeth,' said Hill, only semi-joking. 'Your mouth gets a jolt when you go over it and it is very uncomfortable. You know it is coming but between concentrating on driving and clenching your teeth, it is never enough. They are supposed to have made track improvements but it is not enough.'

It was the same complaint all round with Pedro Diniz talking about making the Ligier less nervous over the bumps, David Coulthard complaining that he had spun on his fastest lap when he hit a bump and Gerhard Berger labelling the condition of the track as 'very poor'.

The Austrian also had other problems with the track in the shape of a German Shepherd dog which appeared in front of him as he hurtled into the Ascari bend in the morning. 'The dog was looking into my eyes,' said Berger, making light of a potentially serious incident.

'If I had been Schumacher, I would have stopped to pick it up and taken it back to Germany with me.'

Heinz-Harald Frentzen went as far as to describe the surface as 'dangerous' after having to change the undertray on his damaged car and Williams' technical director Patrick Head said that the changes since 1995 had made things worse. Speaking at the end of the Friday session, he could not hide his admiration for Schumacher, saying: 'Ferrari seems to be up and down and it was very exciting watching Michael's driving. It reminded me of rallying.' He nominated Benetton as the strongest challengers because they also had Renault engines and had very good engineers and drivers, Berger and Alesi. Ferrari, he believed, while impressed with Schumacher's driving, had a lot of work to do in order to be quick on the more conventional European circuits.

Schumacher went off to see officials to demand that they get some work done to flatten the bumps while Villeneuve said: 'The track is fine but there are two or three spots where there are huge holes and if you go over them at the wrong spot, the car bottoms out and you get a jolt through the spine. I went through twice and now I have a headache.'

The biggest headache for the field was Hill who again demonstrated how much he and the car were in command, moving like a man plugged into a confidence system but he was as wary as ever. Mention of beating or at least equalling Nigel Mansell's five successive wins to start off his 1992 title-winning season was treated with extreme caution.

'That has honestly not occurred to me,' he said. 'What has gone before will not affect the outcome of this race and that is what I am focusing on. Things are going well. The break I took in Rio was fun and I intend to continue enjoying myself here.

'I have won three races in a row from Australia at the end of last season and then odds get higher that something will happen to end the run. I won here last year and I want to do the double. The time is right, for the Williams car is superior at the moment but it will not last forever.

'We have worked hard at improving in areas where we were criticised last year, such as getting the car in and out of the pits quickly, stopping at the right places and at the right times in the race.'

As he tried to stifle over-enthusiasm, his former team-mate David Coulthard, who had lost his seat to Villeneuve at Williams, was attempting to talk himself up again. His start to the season had been less than agreeable but for one delicious moment in the morning session he was top again but finished the day eighth.

'I know there are people questioning my ability but that has not changed since I was doing well against Damon last season and I have no doubts about myself,' said the Scot.

Benetton were trying to find 25 horsepower which they reckoned they had lost from the previous year's car, but when they all rolled out for qualifying on a hot, sunny, windy Saturday, they were all looking for Hill and rightly so, although he kept the best for last.

Schumacher set a flying lap halfway through the session and it looked good enough to last until the end. Villeneuve, who had done little except learn the track all weekend, suddenly got up to second place 20 minutes from the end. Schumacher bettered his time as the clock counted down but with only two minutes left, Hill ventured out and on his second lap ripped past the top time.

'It is a fantastic result for me,' declared Schumacher. 'I would have been very surprised to be on pole.'

'It was always close,' said Hill. 'We left it late to go out and I was biting my nails – as much as you can sitting in a car with gloves on. There was a lot of traffic out there but you had to try to find some space and get in a quick lap and, fortunately, I did.

'It is a tricky circuit to set the car up for. It is very difficult to keep on the track, it is very slippery, especially off the line. Apart from those big bumps it is OK but when you go over those, you really rock and lose sight of the corner.'

Schumacher, still fighting with his car, admitted bluntly: 'For me it is a nightmare. I am really working hard in the car to keep it on the line but it is very difficult with the way it is handling. The real issue will be the track temperature – when it goes up it will get a lot more slippery.'

What changes would he like to make to the car, he was asked. He looked at the questioner, smiled and to laughter replied: 'The press conference is too short. When we get back to Europe we have a lot of issues we can work on in testing. We have a lot of time to sort out the car and we can go in to the wind tunnel to find out what is wrong.

'One thing is that we have cars in the field with two different types of side protection and we will try them and see which is best for us.'

'Diniz in the Oven'

Easter Sunday dawned as a sunny, blue-sky day but with a cool edge which made it pretty damn perfect for racing. A short ceremony before the race marked the memory of the great Juan Manuel Fangio, who had died since the last Argentinian race.

When the lights went out, Hill blazed away off the start line with Schumacher chasing but Villeneuve blew his third place, dropping to ninth as he fumbled with the clutch. He compensated by passing four men in four laps.

They pounded on, bouncing over the bumps, until a double accident changed the fortunes of several drivers. The safety car emerged on lap 27 after Luca Badoer collided with Diniz and his yellow Forti flipped upside down. The cars joined the procession and Diniz, who had been in for repairs and taken on some fuel, rejoined on lap 29 but the car's refuelling nozzle had failed to close and when he touched his brakes, petrol spilled out onto the hot engine.

In the blink of an eye, the rear of the car exploded in flames, Diniz spun the car and the wind fanned the blaze over him. He was obscured by the fire but then he emerged, running from the inferno which burned out the Ligier.

The heir to an £800 million supermarket chain was unscathed, apart from a slight burn on his left hand. His helmet was black from the fire but the £650 he had invested in his fireproof clothing will never be bettered, no matter what the family fortune is. The *Sun* came up with a classic headline, 'Diniz in the Oven', to accompany the photograph of the blaze.

Hill had built up a 10-second lead but now it had gone;

Schumacher was on his tail again and we all waited for another bout of high-speed duelling as in 1995 which saw them end up in the gravel. The new, mature Hill had other ideas and when the safety car, a too-slow Renault Clio, disappeared, he floored the throttle and was gone.

'It was frustrating to see a lead like that evaporate in seconds,' admitted Hill, 'but it was the right decision. It just made me all the more determined to put the hammer down and do it all again.'

Schumacher hung close for a couple of laps – too close, in fact – as it turned out, for Hill's car kicked up a piece of debris which just missed Schumacher and smashed in to the Ferrari's rear wing.

'I saw something black flying towards me and instinctively ducked,' said Schumacher. 'I thought it was going to hit me in the face. Soon after the car got loose and I knew something was wrong.'

He pitted for good on lap 46 and by then ten cars had gone, burned out, clapped out or driven out. Hill's pit-stop went beautifully and he swept to victory while Villeneuve, with a little help from Alesi stalling in the pits and Berger breaking down, made it a Williams 1–2.

A huge hug from his wife as he stepped from the car started the celebrations and Hill could only laugh as he was handed a gift of a giant chocolate Easter egg, for two days of diarrhoea had limited what he could eat to a minimum before the race. The laugh came easily for he was thrilled at overcoming the odds to win his third race of the season.

'It is a fantastic result for me and the Rothmans Williams Renault team,' he said, remembering to give the sponsors their place. 'To win the first three races is just a wonderful feeling. It is a great result for the team to get a 1–2 finish. It is wonderful for everyone who has done so much. That represents the force we are at the moment.

'Michael Schumacher was as tenacious as ever, always looking for an opportunity but I felt I always had his measure. Then the safety car came out. We did quite a few laps behind it and the problem was that it was going very, very slowly and the tyre pressures were going down. That meant that going over the bump in the first quick corner was worse in the first few laps.

'I think the safety car was an excellent decision, very wise. Any time a car is upside down and the driver is having difficulty getting out, you should get the safety car. It did not upset my strategy. I was able to keep pace by keeping a watch on Michael. There are a few places where you can see across from one side of the track to the other to see where the train of cars is behind. I just adjusted my pace accordingly to try to keep the cushion.

'There was a different pressure for me here, it was a different kind of race from Brazil. I have to thank my trainer, Erwin Gollner, for my fitness. I have not been able to eat for two days.'

For those who did not understand, Hill provided a graphic description which even those who speak Chinese or Mongolian could comprehend by helpfully adding with hand movements: 'It goes straight in here and straight out here.

'I am very pleased to have made it through the race without any mishaps and have no ill-effects. Now I have the kind of lead I wanted but would not have dared to assume I would have after Australia, Brazil and Argentina.

'It will be nice to go back to Europe with thirty points but there are many threats to me. Benetton, Ferrari, Jacques. They are all working hard to get back at me and I will have to do as much to keep ahead.

'The car was perfect today. The only problem I had was that the radio did not work so I did not have any way of communicating, so that was a little difficult. I had to rely on the pit board but it was hard to ascertain what was going on.'

Hill was unstoppable and it gave rise to the best headline this year to describe his achievement, from the *Autosport* magazine: 'Serial winner strikes in Argentina.'

Villeneuve seemed to accept that his poor start was due to human error rather than mechanical failure, saying: 'I don't really know what happened. I did not release the clutch enough and it was slipping for a long time before it grabbed and by then a lot of cars had gone past . . .'

The fitness regime Hill now followed and to which he credited his extra energy was a subject to pursue, for while he had always been lean now he did appear to be stronger and equipped with added stamina, allowing him to operate at peak power for longer periods.

'I have trained harder and better over the winter,' revealed Hill. 'I have a gym at home in Dublin now so I can train regularly without having to organise to travel somewhere therefore taking more time out of my life, away from the family.

'I am enjoying it and it worked out well that I spent time in Rio with my trainer last weekend so keeping my training programme going. I had planned a few days' holiday away but when that fell through, I phoned Erwin and asked him if I could join him in Rio for the time up there and he was delighted.

'It was a nice combination of time off and training and I really do feel the benefits over last year. I feel quite a lot sharper this season and as I have not been able to keep anything in my stomach for the last forty-eight hours, I was not able to really restock on carbohydrates or pastas – but I feel very good considering.'

Gollner, who had worked with the famed Willy Dungl clinic in Austria, where many drivers over the years have gone for rebuild or rehabilitation as well as regular fitness workouts, was the perfect fitness adviser. He had worked as a mechanic on leaving school and had ridden motorbikes, so he understood some of the demands on riders and drivers as well as having an appreciation of speed.

Schumacher had long been regarded as the fittest driver on the grid, working fiercely hard in the gym, riding his mountain bike at circuits, sticking to a rigid diet. One night as I drove along the section of the Spa track which is the public road to Stavelot, I was forced to swerve at the last second to avoid a darkly dressed figure in the dusk pedalling furiously along with no light on his bike. It is the only time my reactions have matched Schumacher's.

Gollner was impressed by the German but not enough to join the Schumacher team, for after the Williams outfit had been in touch with him and he had agreed to join the team in November, a bigger offer had come from the world champion. Schumacher had surprisingly dispensed with the services of his physio, fitness and dietary expert, Harry Hawelka, and was looking for a replacement. Gollner was gratified but not tempted and had gone to work with Hill almost immediately, visiting him at his home in Dublin with the driver going to Austria for some work in the mountains.

'We are not yet at the level Damon will be at by the time we get to Hockenheim in July,' he said. 'Fitness is not something you get in just two months. He is keen and we are working hard.'

And he insisted: 'It is not important to be the fittest out there. Damon is a brilliant driver and it is about how he feels in himself. You do need to be fit, of course, very fit to drive Formula One cars with the heat, the long races, the stress and the g-forces.

'Normally after a race you are tired and you have a few days of relaxation but I was very happy when Damon told me the São Paulo race was not hard for him and he did not want to relax. In Rio we would breakfast at about 8.30, then run on the beach, then do some interval work – running for three minutes, one minute exercise doing as many sit-ups, pull-ups as possible. We would do that for 40 minutes. We would have 30 minutes in the hotel gym, 20 minutes of stretching, then go to the swimming pool for some relaxing. Lunch, some tennis, a lot of exercise in the day. It was good.'

Gollner had also worked out a new diet for Hill, adding pureed bananas to his circuit diet, soft cooked rice, pureed potato, lots of soft food which is easier on the digestion, plenty of vitamins and magnesium.

Hill had now equalled Stirling Moss with sixteen victories and he was delighted. 'I share the same birthday with Stirling and it is fantastic to have managed to win as many times as such a great driver. Statistics are a way of gauging how good someone is and so this is meaningful. It is great but I am just very, very grateful for the opportunity to win races in a great car.'

He looked around: 'It can't get any better than this, can it?' and the championship table agreed:

Hill 30 points
Villeneuve 12
Alesi, who had finished third, 10
Irvine 6
Hakkinen 5
Schumacher 4

Schumacher took home the dog, but it was Hill who had proved he had the 1996 pedigree.

Race 3: Argentinian Grand Prix

Result	Drivers (overall)	Constructors (overall)
1. Damon Hill (GB)	1. Hill 30	1. Williams 42
2. Jacques Villeneuve (Can)	2. Villeneuve 12	2. Benetton 13
3. Jean Alesi (Fra)	3. Alesi 10	3. Ferrari 10
4. Rubens Barrichello (Bra)		
5. Eddie Irvine (GB)		
6. Jos Verstappen (Hol)		

5

Hill Loses His Grip

European Grand Prix, Nürburgring: 28 April

Even before Hill arrived in Germany, Schumacher had fired a salvo which appeared perfectly timed to try to unsettle him. The world champion had named the six best drivers in Formula One – and there were no prizes for anyone guessing that Hill was not among them. In no particular order, he named Jean Alesi, Mika Hakkinen, Eddie Irvine, Heinz-Harald Frentzen, Rubens Barrichello and Mika Salo. In 1995 his list had included David Coulthard but no Salo and Schumacher insisted that his judgement was based on drivers who were born to be quick immediately.

'Hill has improved a lot,' he said somewhat patronisingly, 'and he is a very good driver, but he tends to make mistakes under pressure. I think the reason may be that he did not have much experience before he came into Formula One. Drivers who do have a better idea of what is possible in a fight.'

Hill came to the Nürburgring laughing off the comments. He had refused all along to dwell on the Hill v. Schumacher situation and preferred to look forward to victory as he had done in an interview which sparked such headlines at home as: 'I feel invincible.'

At a Williams test at Jerez in Spain where he had added to his season's honours by being quickest by a mile against his team-mate, Villeneuve, the Benettons, Saubers and McLarens, Hill relaxed and contemplated his chances of joining Jack Brabham, Jim Clark and Nigel Mansell as the only men to have won five races on the trot.

'I know the odds are stacked against me but I will never

have a better chance. You dream of something like the start of the season I have had but you don't put too much weight on those dreams. To realise it is a tremendous bonus and when things go this way, you feel invincible.

'I feel I am driving better than I have ever done,' he confessed.

He could also savour the comments of his boss, Frank Williams, a hard man to please, who had given him a glowing reference. After Argentina, as we sat in the Williams offices, he offered his support and admiration for the big improvement in his driver's performances.

'He was in a class of his own, wasn't he? I had no idea he had not been feeling too great but he looked remarkably good after a race like that. The credit must go to Erwin Gollner who has done a super job with both drivers. He approached us and I was reluctant but Patrick [Head] ganged up on me.

'Damon is so strong and positive now in so many ways. He has improved his appeal and personality. He is on top of the job and I believe we can hold it together after such a great start. It won't be easy, for the other teams will doing everything they can to narrow the gap but we have given ourselves a wonderful beginning before we go back to Europe.'

Hill had arrived back as a lion in Schumacher's den, expecting victory where he waved the flag of surrender seven months earlier. It was dark and dank when he left, now it was sunny and warm, just like his season and he arrived back walking tall, wearing sunglasses, feeling cool.

The Nürburgring is one of the most scenic and romantic motor-racing settings in the world, high in the mountains in the far west of Germany, and, fittingly, Goodyear launched a new wet weather tyre, Monsoon, at the race.

It had deeper, wider grooves to cope with very heavy rain . . . and, of course, for once it was sunny and dry for all three days. That was nice for the thousands who turn the area into a place of pilgrimage, for this is the real home circuit for Michael Schumacher whose fans invade the area.

His home town of Kerpen is close and it was on the Ring that he won his Formula Three title. The fields all around become, like Silverstone, vast colourful encampments with hundreds of columns of smoke drifting from campfires and barbecues at all hours of the day and night.

Alongside it, the legendary Nordschliefe, the old fourteen mile circuit on which they raced Formula One until Niki Lauda's horrific fire crash, remains. I tried a high-speed run round the roller-coaster circuit with its swooping hills, blind bends, stomach-churning leaps over crests of hills through the trees with Norbert Haug, the Mercedes F1 boss who is a former saloon car racing driver.

For a few pounds, you can take your car onto the old circuit and risk joining the regular culling that goes with the price of attempting to take on history. There is no way a modern F1 car would cope and the risk of death and destruction is too great to contemplate – but the new 2.82 miles circuit provides a reasonable test of man and machinery.

Hill arrived at the Nurburgring looking a shade more tense than he had been in the first three races. Was it because this had been the scene of a low point the previous season when, in cold, rainy, misty conditions in the mountains, he crashed out? Honourably, he had watched the rest of the race, giving Schumacher a wave as he rushed past on the way to victory and then sat on the steps of a Williams truck and conceded the championship, hardly a startling act as it was wrapped in a German flag after that win. Yet Hill's actions were misconstrued and misrepresented by many in Britain and by some columnists who saw him as surrendering meekly.

In fact, that race became the basis of Hill's rethink on strategy and one change that came of that was that in season '96, interviews would not be conducted with him sitting down looking up at the cameras, a psychologically bad view of someone being looked down on at a time when he looked tired and despairing.

Now he was the dominant figure in all respects, winner of the last four races including the final Grand Prix of 1995, driving with utter confidence in a car which was a class above the rest.

He was in relaxed mood as he sat around contemplating a

hectic schedule which saw the European race and the San Marino Grand Prix back-to-back, upbeat enough to declare: 'Eight days from now, I hope everyone will be sick of my face.'

The idea was to win both races and he seemed in the mood. 'For the last couple of races I have managed to send the German fans home happy,' he said with a grin, alluding to his two failures to finish at Nürburgring and in the German Grand Prix at Hockenheim.

'This time *I* hope to go home happy. This is close to where Michael lived and last year a huge crowd turned up in terrible conditions so he will have massive support again. He will want to do well here. There is every reason to believe he will eke more out of the car than he already has.

'There is talk of 180,000 here and he won't want to let them down. It irked slightly that many referred back to the Bad Time at Nürburgring but there was no escaping the subject.

'Last year the sad thing is that we were in a much stronger position than we realised here. We made a very good call on the grid to change the set-up and strategy which put us a stop ahead of Michael. Whatever happened we would have finished ahead of Michael so it was doubly tragic that I did not get through to the end of the race.

'If I had known that at the time I would have been in a stronger position to drive more conservatively and I could have stayed behind Alesi for a bit longer because Michael was making two stops to our one.'

He reflected briefly as he sat around on the Thursday at the motor home talking to several journalists. 'It is a bit of a shame but this is a different season altogether. Got any good questions?'

Was that the low point of the season? He laughed: 'No. We managed to get a bit lower. By the time of Nürburgring the championship was a mathematical chance. I recognised that Michael had realised the opportunity and grasped it in both hands in determined style. It was a great race.

'What I said after was that I could and should have won – but that is history now.'

Ringing the Changes

The 2.8 mile circuit was busy even for the Friday practice session and the Eifel mountains were soon echoing to the traditional sounds of Damon Hill racing round fastest, morning and afternoon. 'We have successfully set up the car to keep it right at the peak of its performance,' declared Hill, 'but there is still work to do.'

His confidence was not misplaced and in qualifying on Saturday, he dominated with ease to secure his third successive pole position, the fourteenth of his career, with a lap which took him seven-tenths of a second quicker than Villeneuve who was again hampered by not knowing the circuit in his first season, and a massive 1.2 seconds faster than Schumacher.

The continuing delightful weather continued to surprise the drivers but at the pole position press conference Hill's mood seemed less sunny, a touch reluctant as the questions flew, a return to less assured times when he looked suspiciously at those around.

'We are trying to get the maximum out of the car,' he said. 'We found a little bit more at the test in Jerez after Argentina, but not a lot. Conditions are slightly different here but not a lot. I am surprised at the weather, it is superb. I don't know the forecast for tomorrow but I don't mind which way it goes – I am happy with the car.'

What had they been testing, what extras were coming for the FW18, he was asked. 'Those things we have tried will come through later in the season for we are still looking to the future because we know things will move on. We did find a few little things we can use here.

'We are enjoying a period where everything is going superbly well and the atmosphere in the team is excellent but you must keep looking ahead.'

Alongside Hill sat Villeneuve and Schumacher and if the other Williams man was equally satisfied, the German was again listing a series of changes to the Ferrari, mentioning alterations to the suspension and gearbox. Just little steps we are talking about, he said. There was, he insisted, light at the end of the tunnel.

'We are 1.2 seconds behind Damon but we expected that here,' said Schumacher, adding that the circuit suited the Ferrari more. But the paddock was buzzing with talk that the Italian team was again in turmoil – Schumacher was fed up, British designer John Barnard was for the chop by Ferrari president Luca di Montezemolo who blamed him for a poor chassis.

Schumacher exuded patience and diplomacy, perhaps remembering the £35 million two-year contract in his vault. 'I knew when I came to Ferrari that things were going to be difficult and different,' he said, as Hill sat alongside and enjoyed the spectacle of his great rival taking the heat.

'I am still in the second row and in third position. Compared to other teams we are doing a reasonable job. I see light at the end of the tunnel, I don't have a reason to feel frustrated.'

He felt confident that things would improve and that by mid-season they would be winning and thereafter winning regularly. Not surprisingly, Hill did not look worried and no one rushed out to put money on this latest prediction.

It was easier to believe Williams' technical director Patrick Head on the subject of Hill when he said: 'We all got a bit of a drubbing last year and had our noses rubbed in it every two weeks as we looked to our side of things in terms of reliability and strategy and I am sure Damon went away and did his own bit of analysis.

'He's got a confidence about him now. He does not get uptight or appear so fragile if things don't go right.'

Their increased performance was down to improvements by team and driver and limited competition and he was not about to put a percentage on those elements.

Hill was quizzed on the changes he had made around him in support team, new attitude, now being noticed by foreign reporters but he was not too forthcoming, saying simply: 'Well, I did not win last year so I thought I had better change something. It seems to be working.'

Could he be more expansive? 'No, that's all I am going to say,' he replied.

Bad Start

On Sunday warm-up, it was no surprise to anyone that Hill again was fastest. A walkover win seemed a certainty in the afternoon. As Williams basked in the glow of their own brilliance, Montezemolo tried to calm the Ferrari rumours, insisting that all was well, denying that the team might even fold if success was not forthcoming this year.

At the previous race, Villeneuve had blown his start. Now, to everyone's surprise, it was the turn of Hill when the red lights went out. As his car wheels spun impotently, Villeneuve flew past and, amazingly, so did David Coulthard who had gone from sixth to second with the kind of start that dragsters usually make.

'The right revs, the right amount of wheelspin and away you go,' said the Scot later with a smile. How Hill would have loved such a launch. Instead, he found himself fifth behind Schumacher and Barrichello until lap 6 when Hill overtook the world champion.

'It was the high spot of my day,' he said later, while Schumacher lamented a mistake which opened the door. Already Jean Alesi was out, victim of a slow start caused by a handbrake problem, he had pushed to catch up and paid the price with a desperate overtaking move which ended in disaster.

Hill began attacking Barrichello but the Jordan–Peugeot combination handled well and he was held off until suddenly the Englishman began to feel that there was something wrong with his car.

'It felt as if there was a puncture or the anti-roll bar was broken. It felt strange,' complained Hill who stopped on lap 22, earlier than planned, to allow a check which took almost 21 seconds, dropping him down to eleventh place.

Villeneuve was pressing on unchallenged and his stop on lap 26 was quick enough to get him back out into the lead but now Schumacher was beginning to fly, finding a new set of tyres working well for him. The French-Canadian had the opposite problem for his new tyres were not quite as good and he found the car sliding more.

Schumacher closed in with indecent haste and, with 30 laps still to go, he was right behind car number 6 and looking for a way past. Villeneuve settled into a fast but neat series of laps, using the full power of the Renault engine and the handling of the Williams to their best to keep Schumacher at bay.

Much further back, Hill was terrorising the neighbourhood with some lively laps, powering through to eighth and looked to be able to salvage his day... until he met up with Pedro Diniz on lap 28. The two scraped paint and carried on but Hill was less than impressed with the Brazilian. He stopped on lap 42 of the 67-lap race and was up to fifth until he eased past Barrichello and began closing on Coulthard whose McLaren team-mate Mika Hakkinen had shot himself in both feet by twice speeding in the pit-lane and exacting stop-go penalties.

Villeneuve stayed ahead through the pit-stops and although Schumacher looked up the inside, down the outside, feinted various passes, the 25-year-old Indycar champion kept his nerve and got home for his first Grand Prix win.

He had been a wide-eyed boy the last time a Grand Prix crowd had cheered a Villeneuve, his father Gilles, who had won fifteen years before in Spain. Now the boy was the man, the hero and he revelled in the status and the way he had won the race, holding off such a driver as Schumacher.

'I prefer to win my races with a fight,' he declared. 'I don't think I was there the last time my father won but that is not important. I am proud to be my father's son but I do not have a great interest in that. I do not do it for him, but for myself.

'The first win in any series is important but when I wake up in the morning, I will be thinking of the next race. There was huge pressure from Michael and I could not afford to make any mistakes. A couple of times he got very close, too close for comfort – but it was fun.'

Less fun was had by Alesi who was fined £8000 for leaving the circuit without permission after disobeying a marshal after crashing. His team was also fined £6500 to cap a miserable day.

Hill never did squeeze past Coulthard and had to defend himself from Barrichello behind, all three cars separated by less than a second at the chequered flag.

His run had finally come to an end. No famous five for now, no ten points and few smiles. 'I got a ghastly start. I did not get on the clutch point right. I do not blame the car, I messed up the start and the car got bogged down. I am not very pleased. It is the same thing that happened to Jacques in Argentina but it was a poor start and I cannot say I am too happy with that.

'I had to force my way through after that and the car was OK until it came to getting past Michael. I felt there was trouble at the back. I could not get past Rubens [Barrichello] and the car was handling as if it had a puncture. I tried to get used to it but then had to pit.

'That took a lot of time while they checked the rear of the car. After that I was just chasing, trying to make up places and see if I could get a place on the podium. I had a great race with David Coulthard but he was not going to let me past easily. I did not have the straight line speed to get past.'

Coulthard had worked it out and was delighted to take third place, especially against his former team-mate, as he confirmed: 'We had a great battle but I knew that Damon was not going to do anything silly after getting back to fourth. When I saw him behind me eight laps from the end I thought I would not be able to hold out but I made my car so wide that you would not have been able to get by on a motorbike.

'The only way he was going to get past was by going over the top.'

Hill had a swipe at Ligier's Pedro Diniz who had forced him wide at one point, saying: 'These guys won't move over. I don't know why he did not look in his mirrors. It was a race I could have won but things did not turn out that way. It is a damn shame but I messed up the start and the car got bogged down. That's when the problems began.

'It would have been a waste not to get points but that was

not uppermost in my mind when I was behind David. I gave it my best shot but there was an oddity about the car.

'I am pleased for Jacques' first Grand Prix win and I am confident that we are going to be strong at Imola. This was a setback – but these things will happen. I still have my self-belief.'

Race 4: European Grand Prix

Result	Drivers (overall)	Constructors (overall)
1. Jacques Villeneuve (Can)	1. Hill 33	1. Williams 55
2. Michael Schumacher (Ger)	2. Villeneuve 22	2. Ferrari 16
3. David Coulthard (GB)	3=Alesi 10	3. Benetton 13
4. Damon Hill (GB)	3=Schumacher 10	
5. Rubens Barrichello (Bra)		
6. Martin Brundle (GB)		

6

Hill Hits Back

San Marino Grand Prix, Imola: 5 May

Hill suddenly found himself switch from hero to hapless in some corners of the media after the Nürburgring and the reaction to failure in one race was savage. His error, despite winning the previous first three races of the season, appeared to unleash the apparently pent-up feelings of distrust and frustration that linger in many people.

One newspaper likened Hill and Schumacher to London cabbies and suggested that if they arrived together, it would be better to take the one driven by the German . . . although if it were a Ferrari taxi, the chances of getting there would be slim.

Another columnist declared that Hill was too old. Somehow that had not seemed a drawback when he was winning. If it had once been a national trait to support effort over success, yet again it had been shown that these were the demanding nineties and only a win would get him back in the good books at the San Marino Grand Prix.

Hill was less than delighted at the treatment meted out to him after one slip-up but he kept his thoughts to himself and let others do the talking. Ferrari adviser, Niki Lauda, with three world titles, was more complimentary.

'He drove like God in Brazil,' said the Austrian. 'He is under no pressure but if nothing serious happens from now on, the championship has already gone his way. Damon was excellent in South America. Williams had a well-made car for this season and that is why they had a pre-season advantage.'

Hill, grateful for the boost, only referred to his critics once

63

when he was asked if he got upset at bad press in some places. 'No, I don't read it,' he said somewhat disingenuously. 'I had some good fish and chips on Monday night and caught a glimpse of a few things in the newspaper that the chips were wrapped in but I did not spend much time reading it.'

He concentrated on a double challenge at the beautiful Enzo e Dino Ferrari circuit at Imola. The deaths of Ayrton Senna and Roland Ratzenberger in that terrible weekend in 1994 would also cast a shadow on the track but the magnificent setting ensures the race.

The *tifosi*, the Italian Ferrari fans, are there in their tens of thousands, turning the Rivazza hill into a human anthill, turning up with pieces of polythene, groundsheets or straw, planks or lengths of plastic to build makeshift dwellings for the weekend. The atmosphere is wonderful all round the 3.1 mile track which climbs to the top level past the terraced olive groves and villas which sit in the grounds. Changes to corners, particularly at Tamburello where Senna died, have taken much of the pace out of what was a very fast circuit and the current batch of drivers are less than enthusiastic about its stop–start nature.

The teams set up at Imola with varying degrees of optimism. Benetton had a dispirited air, Ligier had been rapped by the sport's governing body, the FIA, who announced that the fire at Argentina in Diniz's car had been a result of a wrongly fitted valve. They escaped disciplinary action. Tyrrell Yahama had suffered the indignity of both cars being disqualified from the European Grand Prix results.

Mika Salo's car had been underweight by 3 lbs and Ukyo Katayama, the Japanese driver who once said the most frightening thing he had seen in F1 was a Williams car coming up behind him, had been given a push start on the grid.

Hill, winner of the 1995 San Marino race, knew that the attack could be even stronger this time from Jacques Villeneuve, who had finally reached a circuit he knew from his Formula Three days, and from Schumacher and Ferrari who particularly wanted to do well at their first home race together on a circuit bearing the Ferrari name.

Villeneuve did not pull his punches when he arrived, announcing: 'There are a couple of silly chicanes and they turned it into a typical modern circuit which I don't think is fun any more. For me it is going to be great to be on a track where I won't have to spend the whole of Friday finding my way round. We can start working straight away and that will save time.'

Tense Mood

Friday morning saw heavy rain and although Hill had a trouble-free run, setting second fastest time, trying slicks on the drying track for six laps, he could not match Schumacher. Of course, he did not need to for the free practice sessions had become a proving ground for the different settings.

Villeneuve was fifth when he stopped for lunch and Schumacher was on top but most had saved extra laps for the afternoon when the weather was forecast to be sunny and bright. So it turned out and again Schumacher set the fastest time, 0.7 inside the lap record and just ahead of Rubens Barrichello's Jordan.

The Ferraris provided the excitement for Eddie Irvine spun off and stopped the session for sixteen minutes while his car was moved and right at the end of practice, Schumacher spun into the gravel, aptly at Villeneuve, the corner named after Jacques' late father, Gilles.

Hill, who also had an off-track excursion, was relaxed about finishing sixth and admitted: 'We know where we are. There is a lot more to come. But I think you can expect qualifying to be extremely close. Ferrari were close in Germany and are obviously improving. Fridays are misleading or at least impossible to interpret from the outside to determine what the real state of competitiveness is.'

As he headed to lunch, one reporter who had been hard on Hill shouted after him: 'Are you looking for revenge?' in semi-jocular fashion, referring to getting back at Schumacher for his better place in Germany a week earlier. Hill smiled and before disappearing inside the Williams truck behind the pits, replied: 'Only on you.'

Neither of the Benetton drivers, Jean Alesi or Gerhard Berger, went for times, preferring to work on chassis set-ups but the pressure was on, for over lunch the team principal, Flavio Briatore, admitted life was tough after the divorce from Schumacher.

'There was no way we could or would pay the money he has got from Ferrari. Neither did Williams. We could not afford to keep him. He went to Ferrari but another team bid more. [That was the Marlboro McLaren team.]

'Jean is quicker than Michael in pure speed but that is not so important. One quick lap means nothing – you need consistency. Yes, our results are disappointing. Jean is trying to do too much too soon. He needs to trust us and we need to trust him. Michael Schumacher and Benetton grew up together and it is hard when we split.

'The car is not that disappointing. There is no crisis but we will concentrate on the car for next year if the results do not come after San Marino, Monaco and Spain.

'We had a very long meeting with everyone so that we could all say what was in our minds. Nobody is happy with the results but we are third in the constructors' championship and we can still prove to be the biggest challenger to Hill this season.

'It is always difficult when you lose the driver you have built the team around. We all knew how Michael Schumacher worked and now we have to find new ways for new drivers. It is like getting a new girlfriend – you have to find out what she likes, what makes her smile. It takes time but I am very happy with the drivers we have. There is no question of changing. These are stupid rumours. Jean has not had an easy start but I have told him just to have patience.'

Hill, so aware of slipping up in the technological race, reiterated his warning about pushing on. 'There are one or two things about the car today which concern me but I am happy. We certainly cannot afford to sit down and say that's it, we have done what we need with the car and leave the situation as it is right now. Nobody at Williams would behave like that anyway. Adrian [Newey], all the engineers, Patrick [Head], push like mad and I get on their case as well. We will be here for the week after the race and pushing ahead, looking for more.'

He was in a tense mood, perhaps wound up by the occasion and being faced with some of those who had written him off after the European Grand Prix. When asked what he would do about Friday, a day which had become little more than a test session with little publicity value, he replied:

'I think we should just have qualifying on Sunday. I could spend more time at home, get up at 8 in the morning, qualify at 9, do the warm-up race, then race. Or we could do what we do in testing which is five days of driving non-stop. That is hard work.'

He was fairly short about Villeneuve, too, saying: 'He is right up there, I don't think there is any doubt. He has had to learn three tracks and he did a very good job with those. He doesn't really have a problem adapting to F1. He works well in the team and we get on fine.'

Alongside him in the Friday Five session, where F1 personalities are summoned to face the media for at least thirty minutes at every race, was Ferrari's team director, Jean Todt, who had talked to Hill during the winter about the possibility of saddling up with the Prancing Horse.

Williams were already the team of the season and it was interesting to consider the possibility of Hill as a Ferrari driver. He confessed, too, that he had been intrigued by the idea of driving for Ferrari after several discussions with them the previous year.

'It would have been a challenge', he agreed, 'and who would not want to drive for them?' Although he added: 'We spoke but the thing is that you should not be too romantic about the job and that is what it is. It is difficult not to with Ferrari but nothing came of it. I was flattered to be in discussions so it was not just a rumour, it was a real possibility.'

Saturday was sunny and the morning practice saw Hill faster than Schumacher by three-thousandths of a second, a margin so small as to give nothing away to either driver about how the cars were going. Schumacher had said after Friday practice that he was really happy with the red car, under no pressure to produce a result in Italy and added: 'Williams is out of reach unless Damon makes mistakes. We will be on the pace by mid-season – too late to win the title but ready to win a few races again.'

The battle for pole was fierce but few were surprised when it was Ferrari who emerged triumphant at the end of the 60-minute battle. Hill had set the quickest time of 1 minute 27.220 seconds and that looked good enough to survive until the dying moments when suddenly the crowd rose to salute a searing lap from Schumacher which got him to the top in 1 minute 26.890 seconds.

As he swept round on his final rundown lap, the car suddenly veered off the track after a support on the left rear suspension broke. The car was unable to return and was towed back later with Schumacher riding high to tumultuous cheers for it was the first time since 1983 that Ferrari had managed pole at San Marino.

Hill was philosophical, declaring: 'It was a good, exciting session and I had to throw the car around but I never count on pole position until the very end. It is a great ride round here, chucking it through the chicanes and everything, I really enjoyed it. I gave it my best but Michael's on home ground and I suppose that lifted him a bit.

'Still, I must say it was a real punch in the stomach to see Schumacher had done a quicker lap. It motivates me to pull out an even faster lap next time. Qualifying is important but it does not tell the whole story.

'This sort of circuit bunches everyone up and the competition is close throughout the field. Ferrari have a good set-up, the car looks good and I think it will be tough competition during the race. I want to have a good race and whenever you get on the front row with Michael and Jacques is behind you know you are going to have an interesting time.

'It is going to be a titanic race. It will be hard to win.'

Villeneuve, third, was disappointed not to have managed pole but, in bullish mood, expected to show more of his hand in race trim. Schumacher said pole was 'fantastic' and wondered whether the Williams could do better in the race but he admitted that they would have a less powerful engine than the special they had for qualifying which gave the speed but could not provide consistency for a whole race.

Tip-top Tactics

Hill re-established himself on top in the Sunday morning warm-up and they headed for a showdown in the early afternoon heat. Schumacher arrived to ear-splitting cheers. Once the cars are brought round to the grid, the drivers stick close while the engineers make their last-minute arrangements and the media and guests prowl around.

In the heat, Hill pulled his racing overalls down to his waist but looked relaxed as he chatted to his lawyer, Michael Breen, who had volunteered to hold the sun umbrella over his friend and client. Alesi nibbled his nails and looked nervous, perhaps worrying about yet another failure, for he had crashed heavily at Piratella in the warm-up, wrecking his car and holding up the session.

Schumacher looked as cool as ever, a model of neatness and good manners as he stood watching the Ferrari mechanics working fast and fastidiously.

When the red lights finally released the power, it was that man again, David Coulthard who made a mockery of all the qualifying efforts and words by bulleting off from fourth position to take the lead. Hill took advantage of the situation to push ahead of Schumacher but on the second lap they swapped position when the Ferrari eased past at the chicane.

Ninety-five minutes later the red mountain that is Rivazza exploded like a volcano as Schumacher crossed the line – but it was Hill who stood on a higher peak gazing over the scarlet sea to a world where he is king.

Ferrari fans flowed from the hill, the stands and all parts as soon as Schumacher's stricken car had crossed the line to claim second place. Klaxons filled the air, rockets screeched into the blue sky and fans danced and sang on the track. If he had won, they would probably have dug up the tarmac.

Yet it was 'God Save the Queen' that rang out to remind everyone that Hill had finished 16 seconds ahead of his great rival. It was his seventeenth win, taking him above Stirling Moss in the British drivers' list, a marvellous achievement in a race so perfect for him that it was difficult to believe this was the same man who had taken a battering for his performance at Nürburgring only seven days earlier.

This time there was no mistake in either his tactics or his driving. The masterplan was daring and so clever that even Hill admitted he had a second discussion with the team only ten minutes before he went out to convince himself that it was the right thing.

The plan was to load the Williams Renault with extra fuel, sacrificing some speed to allow him to stay out longer, aiming to let him build up a lead in an out-of-synch run on the 63-lap, 191-mile race, hopefully sticking close to Schumacher who was expected to be on the more conventional two-stop strategy. Hill would be slower at the start but Williams' chief designer, Adrian Newey, was confident it would balance out. That was the theory, but even he confessed: 'I agreed to it and I must say it was brilliant. We thought we might be a bit slow and further behind Michael at his first stop but the car worked very well.'

Hill, criticised for a poor start a week earlier which would have left him stranded in Oxford Street, made no mistake and it was a bonus to get past Schumacher but he could not believe his luck at Coulthard leading.

'I did not want to let Michael through but I did not want to end up in the gravel so I moved aside,' said Hill. 'With extra fuel and a heavy car, I did not want to work the brakes too hard.'

Schumacher now found himself held up behind Coulthard's slower McLaren although the champion admitted that he could not risk a pass as his brakes were on the limit. It was perfect for Hill who never fell more than 4 seconds behind and when Coulthard went to the pits first, Schumacher had the lead for only one lap before he, too, headed for a 21st lap stop. Hill motored on until the 30th lap when he halted.

Hill had established a big lead while Schumacher was in and when he emerged from his stop, he retained the front position. By the time the Ferrari stopped again on the 40th lap, Hill was 25 seconds ahead. The Williams car managed a 9-second halt on the 50th lap and the race was won.

There was also the fastest lap, achieved on the 49th tour of the circuit as he added a few fractions of a second before stopping. By then, Coulthard was history, a victim of hydraulic failure. Heart failure was almost Schumacher's trouble when his right front wheel locked on the final lap in a cloud of smoke and sparks. 'I would have had big trouble if it had happened just a little bit earlier,' he said. 'It just stopped working and I just made it across the line and stopped.'

That sparked a massive track invasion which later cost the organisers a £125,000 fine, for cars were still running. Gerhard Berger, who was third, crossed the line, parked his Benetton and ran to the pits. Ulsterman Eddie Irvine was fourth to make it a joy day for Ferrari and he had to fight to keep his gloves and helmet as he battled to the garage.

Only eleven cars had finished and they did not include Villeneuve. He and the unfortunate Alesi had collided at the start. 'We were level, wheel to wheel,' said the French-Canadian, 'but he just banged into me.' Alesi blamed Villeneuve. Both had driven on after repairs and Villeneuve had a great run from 21st to sixth until his rear suspension failed. Alesi soldiered on, managed to collect a 10-second penalty for speeding in the pit lane and finished sixth.

Hill had not only won but had increased his overall lead to 21 points and was back to his best. A year earlier the team was being slammed for poor tactics but this time they had out-thought everyone.

'I am involved all the way in tactics,' said Hill. 'We have people who work out the strategy and they did a brilliant job.'

Newey, who had devised the plan, explained: 'It is difficult to overtake here. Assuming we were second or worse, I felt the car was competitive. The idea was to stretch out the first stop. We decided that on Sunday morning. That meant six laps' extra fuel, about 20 kilos in weight which represents a loss of half a second a lap. It worked beautifully although David Coulthard getting in front was an unexpected bonus for us as it kept Michael pinned back.

'Our strategies got more of a slating than they deserved last year. We always work things out carefully but different factors affect your plans.'

Hill finished in defensive mood, countering the euphoria over the win by saying: 'The competition is close and that is one reason why it is great to win. We did not have a large advantage. I am out there to do my best for me, the team and the fans and when it comes off, it is great.

'There was a good bit of lateral thinking about strategy. I had to fully believe in it. You cannot afford to have any doubts in the way. We have a points advantage, not a performance advantage.

'I think that Michael Schumacher is a serious threat for the championship. He has every reason to battle it out for his third world title. He has a car which is very good – he admits it himself – and the engine is not bad. If they start using the engine they had in qualifying then we will have to do something extraordinary to beat them.'

The spectre of Schumacher was definitely looming large again in Hill's life but he had one parting line of assurance: 'I am much more comfortable with my place in the sport.'

Race 5: San Marino Grand Prix

Result	Drivers (overall)	Constructors (overall)
1. Damon Hill (GB)	1. Hill 43	1. Williams 65
2. Michael Schumacher (Ger)	2. Villeneuve 22	2. Ferrari 25
3. Gerhard Berger (Aut)	3. Schumacher 16	3. Benetton 18
4. Eddie Irvine (GB)		
5. Rubens Barrichello (Bra)		
6. Jean Alesi (Fra)		

7

Tunnel Vision

Monaco Grand Prix, Monte Carlo: 19 May

Visiting Monaco during a Grand Prix is like being given the chance to dance with an ageing film star: the thrill of the meeting is there but the fading beauty and shuffling pace make you wish you had been there when she was at her sexiest.

The race which has helped to give Formula One much of its glamour image beckoned them for the 54th time but no one who gathered in Monte Carlo had any idea of the most remarkable Grand Prix which was about to unfold on the streets of the old town.

Monaco sticks to its traditions by having Friday off, a hangover – usually literally for most – of the days when partying was as much the reason for going as racing. That rest day allows everyone a free day to enjoy even more of the inflated prices in hotels, cafés and bars as Formula One and its followers pay off any debts the principality might have for a police presence which is close to intrusive.

Good order is the style of Monaco but if that is the standard demanded in the streets it is something that cannot be provided in the cramped pits and paddock areas. The teams, like everyone else, have a love-hate relationship with the old lady as do the drivers who pilot their miracles of modern technology through a maze of streets which defy the cars to do their worst. So tight is space that some teams further down the grid cannot fit in with the rest on the quayside and are therefore reminded forcefully of their status by being forced to park in the overflow area on the road above.

Hotels ask for a minimum five nights' booking even if you

are there just for the weekend and spectators overrun the team areas, finding themselves able to touch the cars for one rare moment of the season. Yet there is still a touch of class and glamour about Monaco. The yachts in the harbour, the casino, the traffic jams with nose-to-tail Ferraris, Maseratis, Rolls-Royces and Porsches are worth seeing.

It is also the race where you can stand close as the cars race past, feel the pain of the noise in your eardrums and fill your senses with the thrill of the experience. The characteristics of the circuit make for a great race: precious little grip on the oily, dirty public roads, slow, narrow streets and tight corners and heavy demands on the concentration of the drivers, as even Schumacher was to discover.

As Damon Hill said on his arrival: 'If you are not impressed by Formula One cars in Monaco, you will not be impressed with them anywhere. It has a different atmosphere which is down to the venue on the sea with the boats in the harbour, the sunshine, the twisty corners. It is unlike any other track we go to.'

Hill was in town for his fourth race in Monaco and his ambition remained the same . . . to win the race his father Graham had won five times in the 1960s.

Schumacher has a flat there, too, having moved from Germany three years ago, but a dispute with the Monaco authorities over the number of days he spent there – and they do get sniffy if the feeling is that their town is being used simply as a tax haven, although it is – and a desire for more space, a garden for the dogs and somewhere for a family to grow up, had encouraged him to buy a mansion in Switzerland.

No fewer than twelve drivers list Monte Carlo as home: Luca Badoer, Gerhard Berger, Rubens Barrichello, David Coulthard, Mika Hakkinen, Pedro Diniz, Ukyo Katayama, Andrea Montermini, Jacques Villeneuve, Giancarlo Fisichella, Johnny Herbert and Heinz-Harald Frentzen.

'At least I can sleep in my own bed,' said Frentzen. Hill was a visitor, not a resident. Most live outside their home countries for tax reasons. Hill had chosen Dublin for quality of exile, most headed for Monaco. Villeneuve was different again, for he had lived there since the family move when his father Gilles left Canada to race for Ferrari in Formula One. After the death of Gilles in 1982, they stayed on. His flat was a stone's throw from the track and he knew the 2.068 miles round the town as a resident but not as a driver of an F1 car attempting to make the journey seventy-eight times.

Hill was determined to make the most of his visit, opting to stay in the Beach Plaza, taking his wife Georgie and one of the children, 5-year-old Joshua who brought his colouring books to keep himself busy.

'I want to try to relax away from the circuit and not be constantly surrounded by motor-racing,' he said.

He and Villeneuve had both been children of the sport, playing around in the background while their famous fathers strutted their stuff, both flamboyant characters, Gilles more so in the car, Graham a legend on and off the Monaco track.

As he sat at the harbourside in midweek, the port still comparatively peaceful, Hill could reflect on his attempts to put his name on the trophy.

'Monte Carlo stands alone,' he said looking across past the yachts to the bustling streets which would be cleared for racing during Wednesday night.

'Drivers are challenged here in a completely different way. You do a ridiculous speed through a dark tunnel, round the street corners. It is exciting, terrifying and the spectators are as close as they can be to the cars and drivers at times. It is a unique experience on tight, twisting streets and it is a big thrill for everyone. Formula One needs Monaco and Monaco needs Formula One. You cannot have one without the other. It demands respect.

'There is glitz, glamour, excitement and it is a bit of an anachronism in respect of what we require in safety terms compared with the other circuits. If you have a problem there is nowhere to go.

'There are still things that can be done to make it safer. There are limits but you won't find a driver who does not want to race here. It carries a great deal of kudos to win at Monaco. It is right up there with Le Mans and Indianapolis.

'It is the jewel in the crown of the championship and it means you are a racing driver of extremely high calibre to win here. The reputation of the place is that it is dominated by the very best and that makes it all the more attractive to win.

'You drive every inch of the lap. It keeps coming at you all the time. It mesmerises you. In the middle part you tend to lose perspective a bit – it can be a strange experience. All the time here you are working. It is mentally tough. You are constantly busy in the car, the work load is very high.'

As Villeneuve also pointed out, there is no real overtaking area and qualifying here was the most vital question of the season.

'It is vital to have pole if you have a serious ambition to win the race,' said Hill. 'I got pole last year and that was as close as possible to the perfect lap for me.

'I am not the only one who has a chance here. It will be interesting to see Jacques adapt here. Jean Alesi likes Monaco as does Gerhard Berger and Michael Schumacher is the strongest threat. Ferrari are not going too badly. If they have their Imola qualifying horsepower it will be tough.

'This place is not hard on engines, that is not a worry, but it is tough on gearboxes and suspension but equipment will not necessarily do it all for you here. You need a bit of luck, a good set-up and things need to go your way. I would dearly love to win but you cannot force it.'

A year earlier, despite pole, Hill had finished a distant second to Schumacher in a race which signalled a disastrous mid-season spell for his championship hopes but this time he was determined to keep piling on the pressure given an even chance with car reliability. Such had been the dominance of Ayrton Senna who won six times in Monaco that Schumacher was the only previous winner of the race on the grid. He murmured about having little chance but everyone believed that he now considered himself to have a chance of winning for a third year in succession if he could out-qualify Hill in the Saturday battle.

Another fight was going on for a piece of Monaco's motor-racing soul – Rosie's bar, a battered, well-worn establishment halfway up the hill between the first corner at St Devote and the casino. The next-door hospital was taking over the ground and Rosie's, where drivers over the years had stopped in for a drink, was faced with closure.

Hill's father, Graham, had made it one of the places where he would entertain from the table top, Jackie Stewart was a visitor, Stirling Moss, too. Senna, who had had a flat in the town, would call in occasionally for a cool drink and Schumacher had also popped in. Adorned with old photographs and posters, splattered with graffiti, this was a living museum but there was no ground available and Rosie was getting anxious. Happily, the bar was taken over and will live on in another part of town.

Hill may not have had time to emulate his dad, no one does in these days of sponsorship demands, de-briefs and following athletic regimes of fitness and diet. For most drivers, fun is something other people have. Hill has his family and this season brought more friends along for company to races.

Monaco's Buzz

The Jordan team chose to brighten the colourful scene by launching their cars with a new hue of gold, a metallic colour closer to the livery of their B&H sponsors. McLaren were celebrating their thirtieth anniversary, now a massive team compared with the outfit who arrived with a trailer in 1966.

Hill began the weekend in style, leading the way to lunch with the fastest time of the first free practice session. Villeneuve, out for the first time on the streets in an F1 car, had a gentle drive to be eighteenth.

Coulthard, Schumacher and Frentzen all had spins but after the break, Coulthard and team-mate Hakkinen boosted the

McLaren celebrations with first and third fastest times. Hill was sandwiched in second, a contented man, and Villeneuve crept up to seventh.

'I was happy with that,' said Hill. 'We know where we are with fuel and we had a good morning and afternoon – but you cannot afford to be complacent. I did not bother with new tyres. There is 1.5 seconds to be gained by that but it was not necessary for us.

'The idea is to keep people guessing in this session. In the past, when this was the first part of qualifying, you would run to maximum pace. Now it leaves everyone wondering what other people are up to. It is a race set-up test session. You cannot get too carried away, however. Last year we had a good qualifying set-up to get pole then not such a good race.'

He had begun thinking about Monaco immediately after Imola, trying to run the race in his head, remembering corners and the feel of certain parts, for it is a key race in the season.

'It is a difficult place for a driver with all the hustle and bustle,' he said watching the crowds strolling past the Williams motor home three feet from the quayside. 'Just walking from the pits to the paddock, only a couple of hundred yards, is an ordeal. You try to be cool, think of the lap you have just done, recall the circuit, places to avoid but all the time you have to smile, sign autographs even though you are really working.

'You find yourself thinking about it in bed, measuring the circuit. It is a place where you must be precise. It is unique, nowhere else is like it.'

Golfers and athletes visualise the perfect shot, the fastest run, but Hill admitted with a laugh that he had never done the perfect lap in his head. 'You try to conjure up the sensations in the de-brief after a run.

'I feel good driving the car here, I am really enjoying it. You don't know what is going on elsewhere but Schumacher seemed to be having a problem with the car. I expected him to be higher up than eleventh. McLaren look good, though. I thought they might here. It is significant, though, that for the first time this season Schumacher feels he has a chance of winning a race.

'Qualifying is not a question of having the best car as much as being on form. There are unknown factors. It is not the end of the world if you don't have pole but if you do, the race is in the palm of your hand. Qualifying is going to be exciting.'

Like others, he had had a little spin at Rascasse, the hairpin coming away from the swimming pool, and he admitted: 'I was lucky. It is tricky there and I was lucky not have a wheel off. It got sideways and I just flicked the car round at the last moment. I was waiting for the clunk and expected the rear wheel to come off but it stopped short.

'That was a buzz. Occasionally it lets you off but it will always jump up and bite you. You don't get round here without a few moments which will make your heartbeat go up.'

Schumacher was less encouraged, having gear selection problems and the Friday off looked like being blown, but teammate Eddie Irvine provided a piece of insight on the troubles and on the champion's ways. Before the season the Ulsterman had talked of learning from Schumacher and using that information to beat him.

'Eventually testing is going to start for me,' said Irvine. 'It is another matter whether I am going to be able to best him. This guy Schumacher works flat out. He has a serious relaxation problem – he doesn't know how to do it.'

As usual, Irvine was honest and blunt. Had the Ferrari made much progress since Imola in testing? 'I don't think so, no,' he replied. 'It is frustrating, a bit bad, that I have done only one full test this year. It is all because we keep cracking gearboxes and the factory can only make enough new ones for the races. Once we get the new gearbox for Canada or maybe Spain, the situation may change.'

Bernie Ecclestone, Formula One's power-broker, announced a new digital television deal with a £50 million tie-up with Germany's DSF channel, offering viewers five pay-per-view channels of race, replay, timing, on-car film and pit work. It could only help his bank balance which the *Sunday Times* estimated at £250 million, also listing Ron Dennis at £60 million, Frank Williams at £50 million and Tom Walkinshaw, boss of

TWR and owner of Arrows, struggling along on £40 million and one plane.

Schumacher, who had just bought a twin-engined jet with bathroom and bedroom, had taken to wearing a new-look, squarer helmet which offered better aerodynamic results and a gentler airflow than the conventional 'bubble' lids. His old helmets were much in demand and at a charity auction in Monte Carlo, the famous red, yellow and black one fetched an amazing £24,746. The Bosnian homeless also benefited from £17,766 for Hill's helmet, £6345 for Hakkinen's and £5837 for Coulthard's with over £100,000 being raised in total.

Schumacher was now cautiously optimistic, hinting at improved performance, feeling that another win might be his if he could coax his Ferrari to do the entire race.

'The difference between us and the Williams is not as great as it might have appeared in practice,' he said.

'There is always the chance of three in a row. I did not exactly improve in warm-up but the qualifying will be much closer. I can understand anyone making Damon favourite for this race. He has every reason to be optimistic. The car is very good. I was surprised to be second at Imola but we need to work very hard here to get the car to perform at its peak. I am certainly not ready or willing to give up hope of winning here again.'

The warning for Hill was clear but Schumacher was keen to take out insurance against being wrong, saying: 'I know I said that we would not be winning until mid-season but by that I meant winning consistently like Williams. We have been coming closer to them all season.

'I have tasted success here twice before and I want it again. I am as keen to win this time as I was the first, maybe more now. Damon is right, this place is unique and any driver would want this win on his record.'

Coulthard, who lived nearby in Fontvielle with girlfriend Andrea Murray, was working hard to prove wrong the critics who scoffed at his move to McLaren, judging it to be a bad career decision.

'What is important is what the team bosses think, they

employ you,' he said. 'I knew when I joined that the ultimate test would be how I compared with my team-mate and Hakkinen is held in much higher regard in terms of raw speed than Damon. Whether that is justifed or not will be confirmed during our partnership.'

There was no edge, simply solid self-belief to his comment that had he been in the Williams he would be leading the championship. 'Damon is fitter this season and more confident but so am I. I would have started where I finished off last season, running with him or even slightly quicker in qualifying. With more experience, yes, I could be leading the championship'

Too Early

There had been much talk but the phoney war was worth it for the sixty minutes of qualifying on Saturday were the best of the season so far, a thrilling battle of wits and skills. The weather was dull and cool and seven minutes into the session Hill came out and went top. It was shortlived for then Villeneuve shaved just over a tenth of a second off that . . . then Panis, then Alesi, then Berger, Panis again, Coulthard. Hill was suddenly ninth and Schumacher took over as fastest.

Hill tried another four laps but only improved to fourth. He had five laps left of his regulation twelve and sat in the car, visor up, waiting for a third run. With 13 minutes left, he went top, 1minute 20.866 seconds, only 0.046 faster than Schumacher.

His laps were over and he got out in the garage, towelled down, had a drink and quietly cursed himself – with good reason. With only two minutes left, Schumacher nosed the car out and set off. He was down on time in the first two sectors but blazed down out of the tunnel and through the swimming pool complex to capture pole by 0.510 seconds, a huge margin in F1 terms.

He punched the air with delight as the Ferrari team hugged each other and danced with joy while, on the bankings and streets around the circuit, his fans roared their pleasure.

Hill smiled ruefully and said: 'When I got out of the car I knew I had gone too early. You cannot afford to watch the last ten minutes. Everyone knew what they had to shoot at. I had a strong feeling it was the wrong time when I went out but I needed to improve my grid position. I got a clear run and took advantage of it.

'The circuit got quicker all the way through. He managed a good lap so I shall have to make do with second place. It still gives us a very good chance of doing well in the race.'

His team-mate was a very disappointed tenth and declared: 'I have nothing to say. I have to be quicker in the slow corners, like Loews for example.'

On row two of the grid came Alesi and Berger, at last showing real Benetton form but Coulthard, with two lightning race starts behind him, lurked in fifth.

Red Alert

The rain cascaded down on Sunday and as we sat around, Georgie Hill talked of her support for her husband, while trying to look after the three children and cope with the demands of the sport.

'We met in 1981 and I watched him when he was racing motorbikes so I have come right through it all with Damon. For me, coming to a race is supportive and enjoyment. I came because he is away so much racing, testing or on sponsorship work that it is a chance to see him even if it is just a few hours in a hotel.

'He pops into the motor home during the day but he has a lot to do with engineers, sponsors, etc. He's here to do a job, not to have fun and you have to remember that. I think it is nice for him to have someone around to talk to. Lots of things happen and he likes to talk. He has friends here if I am not and that helps him relax.

'For me it is a relief at the end of the race. It has always been that way. A race is a long time to bite your nails. You get excited if he has gone well, disappointed if not but there is always relief that he is fine.'

Grey lowering skies threatening more massive downpours earned the drivers an extra 15-minute session to test in the rain and conditions were so bad that Hakkinen and Montermini both crashed. Sadly for Montermini, the cash-strapped Forti team have only two cars and there was not time to fix his and so, despite having qualified, albeit 22nd, he failed to race.

Light rain continued as they lined up for the start and the sense of anticipation was high in the vast crowd which had poured into the tiny principality and now filled every vantage point all the way round, standing on balconies of hotels and houses beneath which they would race, packing Casino Square, sitting almost on top of each other in the gardens above the Rascasse corner.

They did not have long to wait for drama. Out went the red lights and Hill gunned the Williams past a faltering Schumacher whose Ferrari spun its wheels before gripping a moment too late. Hill led into St Devote, a bent elbow of a corner taking the field uphill parallel with the east side of the harbour towards the casino.

Hill poured it on to establish a gap but he need not have bothered for as he looked in his mirrors heading into the tunnel, he must have wondered why they were not filled with red. Unbelievably, Schumacher was by then climbing from his damaged car, out of the race inside a minute. He had put the right wheel on the kerb at Portier just after Loews hairpin and then hit the guardrail. 'I made a mistake at the start and then I made a mistake in the corner. I am very sorry for the team. I am very angry with myself.'

He was the biggest name to disappear but certainly not the last. Jos Verstappen paid the price of a gamble on slick tyres by lasting only until the first corner when he went straight on. Amazingly, the two Minardi cars had also lasted only a couple of hundred yards before they crashed – into each other.

As Pedro Lamy and Giancarlo Fisichella walked humbly

back, blaming each other, their boss fumed, saying: 'We plan
the race in detail and it is annoying to see everything wasted
by unbelievable mistakes by our drivers.'

Rubens Barrichello was hit from behind in the Square and
lasted only until Rascasse where he hit the barrier. One lap,
five fallers and Hill off on a cruise was four seconds ahead of
Alesi after it. By the start of the sixth lap Hill was 13.3 seconds
in the lead and, remarkably, eight cars were out.

Back in the pack, Olivier Panis began to move up from
twelfth but the rest of the field was in a train behind third-
placed Irvine who was grinding along. Frentzen was behind
the Ferrari and growing impatient as there was no sign that
Irvine would be blue-flagged and told to move aside. Inevitably,
he did have a lunge and damaged his nosecone as Irvine
slammed the door in his face. It cost Frentzen valuable time in
the pits. None of this mattered to Hill who was lapping up to
4 seconds faster than anyone else.

Hill lapped Luca Badoer by the 16th trip round the town
and on lap 28, with the streets drying, he headed in for slick
tyres with a 25-second cushion from Alesi. He emerged behind
Alesi and then swept past the Frenchman two laps later on
the way past Rosie's bar, real name The Chatham Bar.

Soon his lead was 26 seconds and it looked as if he would
have time to stop at Rosie's and do some table top entertaining
of his own before finishing. But as he flashed through the
colourful streets on lap 40, Hill suddenly saw the colour he
dreaded in the cockpit. It flickered on and he looked again
and again, mesmerised by the red light. Something was wrong.
He told the pits and they began checking but even as they did,
the red light glowed in the dark of the tunnel under the casino
on lap 41 and he ran out of luck and oil.

Out of the tunnel he came with a lick of flames from the
back of the car, a pall of blue smoke. Immediately he hit the
brakes and pulled up in the escape road. Down below, around
the port and at the pool, they watched as he sat in the car and
then got out slowly. He banged his helmet in frustration with
both hands and began the long walk down to the pits. Later it

was found that a 50 pence part, a seal, had come loose allowing the oil to spill out from the engine.

He got the cheers of a crowd who recognised that this man had been cruelly robbed of his inheritance without making a mistake. I left the media room and met him as he made his way along the quayside to the Williams motor home.

'I am just disappointed,' he said in resigned tones. 'There was nothing that could be done. I knew there was a problem for a lap before but I don't know what caused it to fail. I have to accept the fact now that I won't win this race. I was flat out in the tunnel when it went. The engine seized up.

'There was oil all over the track and all over the rear wheels. They were locking up and I just managed to park it. It is very sad. I felt it was mine to win.

'I had no idea what happened to Schumacher. All I knew was that I had a big gap and I wanted to make it as large as possible so that I could make another stop if needed.

'Our strategy was perfect. I would not have stopped again and everything was going beautifully. It is no consolation to know I had done it perfectly. You have got to have reliability from the engine but this is not a very hard circuit on engines. It is a long time since an engine let me down.

'The crowd reaction on the way back was absolutely brilliant. The reaction, the acknowledgement that I was doing a good job at the time I stopped was tremendous. Apart from myself, I am very disappointed for the whole team.'

He had dropped in at the pits on the way past and there were even a few smiles from Hill as he spoke to the engineers. 'We did laugh in the garage,' he said. 'I'm doing my best. I just hope this is not too costly for the championship.' Then he found a little bit of privacy in the motor home where his wife gave a comforting cuddle and a kiss. 'It's a terrible shame,' she said. 'I know he wanted to win it so much.'

Hill saw the finish on television and what a finale. Villeneuve completed a miserable weekend for himself and Williams on lap 67 when he retired from fourth place after being hit by Badoer's Forti which also went out. The Italian was later fined

$5000 and given a suspended two-race ban for the accident.

Most of the drivers watched the finish on television, for by the time the race reached the two-hour limit and was stopped three laps short of the scheduled 75 laps, only three cars had crossed the finish line. Astonishingly the victory went to Olivier Panis, a win for a Frenchman in a French team which thrilled the country and the principality. David Coulthard, who had caused some initial confusion by driving in a Schumacher helmet because his own visor kept misting up, enjoyed some of the champion's success, lighting the candles on the McLaren celebration cake with second spot. Johnny Herbert, in the Sauber Ford was third.

It was a new low, even less than thirty years earlier when Jackie Stewart won at Monte Carlo. It was a new low for Hill, too, but he was determined to put a brave face on it. Instead of flying home, he stayed on for another night to relax but because of the vast crowds which invaded the paddock area, he had to commandeer a boat to escape. Ironically, it was Peugeot who came to the rescue, lending a small power boat they had for the Hills and travel agent Lynden Swainston to sail out of the harbour and round to the hotel to land at the jetty. Even the choppy sea was better than the crowd. It was not the ideal end to the day but Hill was in good enough form later to sign occasional autographs, including one for a small boy who said how sorry he was.

The next day, Hill flew home and among the many celebrities at Nice Airport as they departed after the Cannes Film Festival – Elizabeth Taylor, Cher, Ivana Trump, Hugh Grant – none had a better public face than the racing driver who refused to waste energy by being bitter.

'We can put this disappointment behind us,' he said forcefully. 'We have to get on with the championship. This shows how tough it will be, you can take nothing for granted.'

Yet he could afford to be optimistic for the most bizarre race in F1 for years had not affected the top points scorers, for none had finished.

Frank Williams could sympathise: 'I know how much he

Happier days for Damon and Frank Williams in 1992 when Hill joins the team as a driver.

Four years on: tense times for Hill as he waits to race – and for Frank's decision on his future.

Hill joins the England rugby union front row in pre-season training.

Hill leads from the front as he did for most of the season, starting in Australia.

Splashing his way to victory in Brazil.

The sweet taste of champagne completed a perfect day in São Paulo.

A rewarding
moment as Hill
receives his pole
position award from
Carlos Menem,
President of
Argentina.

Hill leads
from Ferrari on his
way to victory in
the Argentinian
Grand Prix.

Michael Schumacher leads the field at the start of the San Marino Grand Prix as Hill waits in second place on the grid.

Hill cools Schumacher's ambition after winning at Imola.

Through the first corner on the streets of Monte Carlo Hill leads from world champion Schumacher – but both were soon out.

Start of disappointment for Jacques Villeneuve in Montreal as Hill takes the inside lane and the fast route to victory.

Mixed emotions after Villeneuve and Jean Alesi again finish behind championship leader Hill.

Hands across the divide: friendly rivalry continued throughout the season for the two Williams drivers.

wanted to win this race, so I can feel for him. I thought he did a brilliant job. He disappeared early on, drove superbly and it was rotten luck to suffer an engine failure.'

Hill retreated to think about the next race in Spain but if he thought things could not get worse, he was to be proved wrong.

Race 6: Monaco Grand Prix

Result	Drivers (overall)	Constructors (overall)
1. Olivier Panis (Fra)	1. Hill 43	1. Williams 65
2. David Coulthard (GB)	2. Villeneuve 22	2. Ferrari 25
3. Johnny Herbert (GB)	3. Schumacher 16	3. Benetton 18

8

Hill Washed Out

Spanish Grand Prix, Barcelona: 2 June

The hot afternoon sun had the locals moving at energy-conserving pace but in the Formula One paddock at the Circuit de Catalunya, the usual feverish activity was taking place as mechanics unloaded equipment from trucks and the motor homes were set up in readiness for the assault on the senses they call Grand Prix racing.

Hill sat in the shade of the tented area at Williams, having flown in that morning, buoyed by another series of successful tests at Silverstone the previous week when he had come out on top by a considerable margin from Villeneuve. Other teams had been a second behind and his only problems had been a spin and an engine failure as Williams worked on transmission and clutch, but the effect of another expensive round of testing had been to confirm in his mind and the minds of all around that despite what had happened in Monaco, the FW18, V10 Renault engine and Hill were still the best trio on the grid. Yet the Monaco disappointment lingered, the sense of daylight robbery lived on and the atmosphere at Spain is never particularly lively. It is conducive to musing and Hill mused with all of us on the past misfortune.

'In my mind I felt I did a good job but got nothing out of it,' he said. 'I would love to be back in the car going round and leading the race again in Monaco – it was a fantastic feeling. I have a real sense of loss over that race. We could have done with the points apart from anything else. That would have been beautiful.

'It is no good cursing luck. There are ten races left and that's

91

what I have to concentrate on. We are coming to the crunch part of the championship. I know I have been saying that but the next five races are very, very important and we have to focus on those and keep going in the direction we were headed in Monaco.

'I know I have said this too, but I expect increasing competition. Ferrari have shown they are literally going at pace. Benetton and McLaren will get closer in the next two months. It was just luck that none of our main rivals scored points. It was a lucky escape. Everything had gone so well but the bolt that controls the oil pressure system went and the engine ran without oil for about four seconds – it is defunct. I kept my foot down thinking it was a temporary hitch – it wasn't.

'The engine lunched itself. It was a solid mass. Someone pointed out later that my dad had gone up the same slip road in 1964 but then push-started the car and got it going again. Well, this one was not going to go – it wasn't a runner after that.'

Then he was off to do the many things in his mind. Schumacher, presumably, was number-crunching for he was likely to earn over £50 million this year, claimed an Italian magazine, who had counted up his earnings from salary, his Michael Schumacher Collection of casual wear and souvenirs, and his contracts with such companies as Omega and Nike. The figures Hill was worrying about, however, were the statistics for Catalunya. Barcelona has several high-speed corners, offers overtaking opportunities on a long straight and is tough on tyres.

Hill's 43 points, 21 more than Villeneuve, 27 more than he had himself, might also have concerned the German if he still harboured secret thoughts of a sudden revival to give him his hat-trick of titles.

The rarity of a Renault engine failure seemed to have unleashed several lurking fears about the power behind his title challenge and he admitted: 'The reliability of the engine is a concern. There is growing pressure on Renault to produce more horsepower but we do not want to sacrifice reliability.

Given the choice I would opt for reliability.

'There is no doubt that we need to sort something out on the horsepower front pretty soon. Ferrari have made big leaps forward and other engine companies are making big steps. This, for instance, is the sort of place where if you have more power you can drag more wing around and actually use the downforce.

'This is always the problem – if you have got the power you can carry more wing so you can get extra downforce so you are ultimately quicker on the whole lap. There is no substitute for it – you have got to have the oooooomph. Don't get me wrong, the Renault engine is still the best all-round package in terms of reliability, horsepower, versatility and the useable nature of it.'

Nevertheless, it was now accepted in the pits that the Peugeot engine had made big strides and its straight line speed was the best of any. Ferrari's new unit had done the job in qualifying and would be honed to survive a full race and Mercedes were ploughing in millions of pounds to get it right at McLaren.

'If the trend continues, then we will have a problem with straight line speed,' agreed Hill before turning his attention to the job in hand. 'Looking at qualifying here, you would say that there are a lot of people spread over just two seconds, really from 1–12 on the grid. You would need only a small snag in a one-hour qualifying session and you could slip right down the grid. We are still the team to beat here, though.'

Although he had been testing, there had also been time at home, a must, he agreed, for he had escaped from the trap of doing too much work, filling his head with Grand Prix.

'I get the best out of myself when I relax, so I like to get time at home. I am very aware now of taking on too much. Testing, for instance, is important, but it has to be quality, not just volume. I have tried to cut down a bit. I drive well when I look forward to getting in the car. There were times last year when I thought we overdid it on the testing front. It was quite common for me to do six days driving a week, three days at a race, three days in a test. It was too much. You get to the point when you cannot distinguish the valuable from irrelevant things so I would rather not get into that this year.

'I am not trashing myself between races and overdoing it. I am very intent on giving the best of myself every time I am in the car so I have to create those conditions. That is better for me and for the team.'

A German reporter popped up to ask: 'Last year you had a big points lead in the championship and then Michael Schumacher caught you . . .' Hill interrupted him to say: 'You don't have to remind me.' Was he frightened of losing it again? 'I am pretty determined to make sure that it doesn't happen again,' said Hill firmly.

'It is really a kind of meaningless point because when I am leading a Grand Prix I think about winning the race and when I am going for the championship I am thinking about winning that so to say I am frightened of losing it – well, that point does not really exist because all my attention is on winning and not losing.'

He insisted that he had not allowed himself the dangerous daydream of thinking about where he might win the championship. It was like being in the car during a race, he said. As soon as you allowed yourself to think about what the first drink would be at the end, you were exposed to something going wrong.

'I am not even thinking beyond this weekend. In fact, I am not even thinking beyond the end of the day. There is stuff I need to do today and when I do those things, I will then think about what I need to do tomorrow. That's the way I do it really. If I thought about all the things that might happen in a day, I might not get out of bed.'

Engine Fears

Hill's ideas that the competition were close were borne out in the tightest possible way on Friday. In the closing moments before pasta appeared for lunch in most motor homes, Hill went fastest, beating Michael Schumacher's time – by one-thousandth of a second. Blinking an eye takes a lot longer, taking in the difference is a mile race compared to the actual time space between the cars.

The only mishap for Hill, who was not entirely satisfied with his car's handling, was a puncture. With all the teams conscious of saving their tyres on a 4.7 mile circuit which chews them up because of dirt and the nature of its racing corners, the afternoon session changed everything round. At the end, it was a Ferrari first but not Schumacher, it was Eddie Irvine. Naturally, he immediately scorned the reason he was on top, his chances and all who came to see him.

'I haven't a chance of winning. The car is a long way from good. I was struggling until I got new tyres. I don't think you can take any hope from this session. I am still well behind. The best we can hope for is a podium place. Olivier Panis's win in Monaco shows that anyone can do it but a genuine victory for us is still a long way off. The car is very difficult, you have to drive every metre of the track.'

He added for good measure with a smile: 'Anyway, I'm not going to be at the front if you lot are going to come round and pester me.'

His view of the car found sympathy with Schumacher who was fifth. 'The car is not as good here as it was in Monaco where I was more optimistic about winning.' Significantly, he added: 'I do not consider these times to be too important. The cars are not running under the same conditions. It does look as if it will be close.'

Hill seemed the happiest of the lot, pleased to be fourth behind Irvine, Rubens Barrichello and Panis. 'Fridays are fun now. You can play with the car and set it up,' he declared. 'We have a very good basis on which to work to give us some more speed.'

Villeneuve, recovering from his Monaco mauling, was more like his old self, assured, confident, defiant, from sixth position. 'I need to be back on the pace here after Monaco. A 21-point lead for Damon seems a lot but it could be virtually wiped out in two races.

'The championship is still wide open and I think there is still hope for Schumacher and myself, I have not given up and I don't think Damon will expect that he has a free run.'

Hill found there was no such thing as a free run, for in Saturday morning's warm-up he punctured a second tyre, aggravating the shortage as each driver is allowed just seven sets of tyres for the entire weekend. His team-mate managed to get half a second inside Schumacher's winning time in 1995 but then suffered what Hill feared, an engine failure.

There was no problem when the big hour came. Hill took pole with a dominating series of drives. Whatever anyone else did, he did better. He was out after 18 minutes for two quick laps which put him on top but then Schumacher and Villeneuve passed this time. With 18 minutes left, Hill beat those two with a superb 1 minute 20.895 and just to underline his superiority, beat his own record by almost three-tenths in the final minute. He was on top, looking good, back in business. Villeneuve was second, Schumacher and Irvine third and fourth.

Another mention of worry about the engines ensured that he would not win the Renault award for bonhomie that weekend but he was intent on getting his message across that they must move on. It was no less than Nigel Mansell, Ayrton Senna and Alain Prost had done in their time.

'I had an engine blow in testing and Jacques had one here. You have to ask Renault if there is a common factor. We as a team are trying to take steps to ensure reliability. It is something that has been bothering us since the start of the season and Williams and Renault are working hard to solve it. But it is frustrating when you don't see progress.'

There was no lack of desire to fix the problem, he added, but it was bad when there was a recurrence. Villeneuve had been fined $5000 for speeding in the pit lane, but he laughed when he was asked about the engine failure and smiled before replying: 'I did not say any bad words about Renault so I cannot comment.'

Tyre wear was also a problem, predominantly the front left with long, fast corners where a car slides and eats the tyre away but Hill felt confident: 'We are in good shape. It is very important for me to do well here.'

Schumacher, sitting nearby on the pole position press conference, was less satisfied, saying: 'The circuit is not ideal for our situation. We are just too slow.'

Schumacher Superb

With a group of friends Hill headed for a meal not far from his hotel on Saturday night in good spirits but the weather on Sunday morning dampened the mood a touch. Heavy rain had started during the night accompanied by thunder and lightning. That was still rolling around as we drove to the circuit. Roads were awash and flooded, heavy grey clouds cocooned the hills and the lights of the motor homes shone in the gloom. Yet Hill had won well in Brazil in a monsoon and although it was hammering down, there was no reason why they could not find the right set-up to give enough grip with sufficient power to enjoy a steady drive at the front.

That was the theory. How difficult it was became obvious when Heinz-Harald Frentzen had a huge crash when he came round the final bend into the straight and skidded off into a tyre wall, careering along as the Sauber Ford split into three pieces and left him sitting in the cockpit. The doctors examined the unscathed German and the bulletin declared him to be 'in good conditions (sic) to take part'.

The times were 20 seconds slower than in qualifying but as the morning went on, the rain increased. I met Hill on a stairway behind the pits and we were discussing how bad conditions were when he was called away to meet a distinguished-looking chap in a raincoat standing at the bottom with a small group of men.

It was King Juan Carlos, making a quiet trip around the pits. Had it been British royalty, the whole area would have been sealed off and secured but the Spanish King was far more relaxed, chatted to Hill and then enjoyed a lift around the track with Schumacher.

The King insisted: 'I don't have any favourite. Like any sportsman I only hope for a good race and that the best man wins. These cars are real works of art.'

Hill's sights were on dethroning Schumacher as king of Formula One but neither man was particularly regal when they started. Conditions were dreadful and this time Schumacher had a start which he described as a 'disaster', falling from third to ninth although he was back to sixth by the end of the first lap.

'I was really worried that I would be rammed from behind' he admittted. 'The clutch was either 100 per cent on or 100 per cent off.'

Hill's brilliant pole work was washed away as he let Villeneuve and Alesi roar past before he got wound up. He held third until lap 3 when an excursion through the gravel allowed Berger and Schumacher past.

On lap 5, the Ferrari overtook the Benetton and the charge, as relentless as the rain, was well and truly on. He was lapping two seconds faster than the rest and in total command but Hill was like a novice skater, losing it again on lap 8 under braking, dropping to eighth and losing 14 seconds on the leaders.

By now, six cars were out, including the Minardis of Fisichella and Lamy, who had unbelievably repeated their stunt of Monaco and driven into each other at the start. Schumacher was on another planet and riding the famous Prancing Horse as if it were a dry run down the coast road. He outmanoeuvred Alesi, no slouch in the rain himself, and was up to second and closing fast on Villeneuve. There was a feeling of inevitability about the simultaneous incidents shortly after.

Hill came round the last corner and started to spin into the straight. The car hit the pit wall and scraped and bounced along, coming to an undignified halt in front of the jeering Ferrari fans. A crowd of 53,000 had braved the weather and within seconds it was obvious who was most favoured.

As Hill climbed the wall for a short, sad walk to the garage, Schumacher chose his moment to pass Villeneuve at the Seat hairpin where he had taken Alesi and the roar could have blown away the low clouds. By the time they crossed the line on that lap, Schumacher was almost three seconds ahead and the race as such was over, although the fascination of watching someone driving on another level from anyone else held the attention until the chequered flag.

As others such as Irvine and Coulthard lost it and drowned in the cruel sea that was the Catalunya track, Schumacher sailed on, with Hill standing in the rain watching with the pit wall crew. Schumacher made two pit-stops and still had a 64-second lead at the last halt when he could have had afternoon tea and still won. He had finished second in 1994 with the car stuck in fifth gear for a chunk of the race and this time he won with the Ferrari firing on only eight or nine cylinders and a broken exhaust.

For the second successive race, only three cars made it to the chequered flag, three more were classified in the top six and fourteen had spun off or broken down.

Hill changed and watched the end of the race in the Renault motor home where a large television stood in the corner displaying vividly Schumacher's skill. He shook his head and braved it out, speaking candidly of the feeling of driving at high speed in such conditions.

'I feel the race should have been a rolling start with the pace car and I told my crew that before the start. It would have been safer in hazardous conditions.

'I want to say that there is no one to blame but myself. I made three mistakes and had the wrong set-up on the car. It is down to me what happened. I made a bad start and went off twice and the last time I lost it in the corner just where Frentzen had in the morning.

'I am happy just to be in one piece. In those conditions I am almost pleased to be out of it. You could not see the track ahead and if there had been something in the middle of it you would never see them. You are putting your life on the line more than normal because you cannot see. It is not just your own life as much as other drivers. It was very, very dangerous, very difficult to see and I was having problems. I am afraid it was a bit of a write-off.'

The set-up problem was the decision to run the car with a dry set-up, based on the morning warm-up and hopes of improving race weather. That keeps the car running stiffly with less downforce and more speed and acutely responsive to the driver. Hill and Villeneuve had used those set-ups and suffered although the French-Canadian at least finished fourth.

'I was quick this morning and thought I had a good set-up,' admitted Hill, 'but I was in trouble from the start and could not keep up with people. I had the wrong set-up for the conditions. They got worse and it was very difficult.'

He knew the critics would have a field day. 'Schumacher reigns in Spain' was already being written by a headline writer somewhere along with the sub-heading: 'Hill washed out'.

'I reckon I am as good in the rain as anyone so I have to work out what went wrong today,' he said. 'I hope this is not too costly to the championship. It's bound to be.'

That was the same pay-off line as in Monaco but this time damage had been done for his lead was down to 17 points and Schumacher was now level with Villeneuve on 26.

Schumacher's joy was unconstrained. 'I wouldn't have bet a penny that I would win after the results in the rain in Brazil and Monaco,' he said. 'I think the race should have been started by a pace car.'

He does like to list his problems which makes one wonder how he finished and apart from the misfire which cost him 6 mph on the straight, there was the problem with the clutch at the start and the freezing cold in the cockpit. The simple fact was that Schumacher drove one of the most brilliant races you could ever wish to see in conditions which made every driver's efforts an act of bravery.

The result, however, apart from boosting his legend, had also rejuvenated his challenge for the title and he concurred with the idea that it might not now be as impossible as he had predicted earlier in the year. 'Yes, I think I can win the championship,' he said. 'It is wide open and there is still a long way to go. The next two races are very important.'

His mood was good, enough to enjoy some banter and he

quipped: 'The King of Spain was a great help when I took him round the track. I would love to have him at my side for the next race in Canada as I am sure he would bring me luck.'

If it was down to luck and omens, Hill had perhaps shaken hands with the wrong man, David Ginola, the Newcastle United winger who could have told him plenty about having huge leads in a championship and seeing them drift away.

Race 7: Spanish Grand Prix

Result	Drivers (overall)	Constructors (overall)
1. Michael Schumacher (Ger)	1. Hill 43	1. Williams 69
2. Jean Alesi (Fra)	2=Schumacher 26	2. Ferrari 35
3. Jacques Villeneuve (Can)	2=Villeneuve 26	3. Benetton 24
4. Heinz-Harald Frentzen (Ger)		
5. Mika Hakkinen (Fin)		
6. Pedro Diniz (Bra)		

9

Hill Robs Prodigal Son

Canadian Grand Prix, Montreal: 16 June

The smell of fatted calf was in the air as Jacques Villeneuve headed to Montreal and despite the events of Barcelona, Hill was not in the public mind of Britain or Canada, a phenomenon for which he could thank the Euro 96 football tournament and the return of the prodigal son.

'I haven't seen much of Jacques around, where is he?' asked Hill with a smile when he arrived for the Canadian race. He did not know but he was well aware that the vast amount of hype swamping Villeneuve, 1995 Canadian Sportsman of the Year, Canadian Athlete of the Year, had created a short diversion for him. It was impossible to walk the streets of Montreal without knowing about Villeneuve. He was on the front pages, there were special magazines devoted to him, and large cardboard cut-outs of him in racing uniform smiled at you everywhere. The 'Jacquomania' had shifted most of the tickets for the three days as Canadians rushed to see their boy in his hometown.

Hill had stopped off in New York for a couple of days on the way to Montreal where he looked around with some friends and bought a couple of guitars, possibly with his return to the stage in mind at the post Silverstone race party.

'I had never been and I just wanted to see the place,' he said, adding with a laugh,' I don't think they're ready for me yet.' It was a nice little line in self-deprecation and the trip was part of his continuing policy of relaxation before races, freeing the head of F1 fantasies.

Several others, including Johnny Herbert, had arrived via

the Indycar race in Detroit the previous Sunday where they made contacts and cheered on Mark Blundell who had switched from F1 to find a good drive in 1996. Herbert, a 5 ft 6, blond-haired, ruddy-cheeked cheery was a few days off his 32nd birthday but the paddock at Montreal loved the story of how a Detroit bar refused to serve him a beer because he did not have ID to prove he was over 21.

The rumour mill was working hard, grinding out gossip that Williams' highly regarded chief designer Adrian Newey was being lured by several teams, that Mika Hakkinen would replace Jean Alesi at Benetton in 1997, that Martin Brundle would lose his seat at Jordan.

Hill concentrated on the preparation to end a bad run. He had never won at the Montreal circuit, just 2.7 miles long, a mixture of street and permanent track on the Ile de Notre Dame in the middle of the St Lawrence river. Built round a lake it is used just once a year despite the wonderful setting and city backdrop and had a reputation for incident and action as the track could be dirty and very tough on brakes.

While Hill relaxed, Villeneuve was in heavy demand and gave a press conference attended by 120 international media, mainly Canadian and including thirteen television crews and, as usual, he caused some to bridle at his matter-of-fact replies, refusing to give the pat, diplomatic answers. Was he looking forward to driving on the Gilles Villeneuve Circuit, named after his father, winner of the race in 1978? Well, it was not really a special thing because although it had been named after him, he had not designed it.

'I remember when I won a Formula Atlantic race there and everyone said "it must be a special feeling on a track named after your father" but the main joy for me was that I had won in the country of my birth.'

He was proud to be his father's son but he was not his father and not attempting to be so. 'In a way I am sick of people asking me the same questions about me and my father,' he said. 'I never saw him as a race car driver, just as a dad.'

The questions flew, the answers flowed: an F1 car should

be quicker than an Indycar because it was 200 lbs lighter and better in tight corners; Nürburgring was his best race; Schumacher was the driver he rated because he was very aggressive, very competitive in the car; the main difference between Indy and F1 was media pressure; by the end of the pressured weekend he would feel twice as tired as usual.

Labelling Hill evasive, Villeneuve revealed more of his working relationship as he talked of his experience of moving into Formula One and the problems of adjusting technically.

'I came with a fresh approach,' said the 25-year-old. 'Damon and I have completely different set-ups concerning things like springs, shock absorbers, ride-height, anti-roll bars, etc. It would be impossible to transpose settings from one car to another and that does not make life easy for the team.

'Apart from exchanging data, Damon and I rarely work together and this is a situation I am used to. In Formula Indy, even in teams comprising two drivers, both work out of their own trucks. In Formula One, when Damon and I are together, he tends to be quite evasive. I find that normal. Why should he reveal his secrets to me? I would not reveal mine to him and I certainly have more to learn from him than he does from me. Even if I needed his help, he probably wouldn't give it. That's not what he's paid for. He is paid to win. Me too.'

Was his objective to help Damon win the title in the second half of the season or was he aiming for it himself?

'I race for myself and for the team, not to help Damon win the championship,' was the uncompromising reply. 'I can understand that what matters for Williams and Renault is winning, whoever the driver is. However, a driver has got to think of himself.

'In some teams there is a number one and a number two but that is not the case in Williams. Frank Williams does not expect me to help Damon. He expects me to win races, and if possible, the title. If, later in the season, I am not in the running, my position will change but not before then.'

Elsewhere Villeneuve confirmed that they 'did not really work together' but said it was nothing political. Damon had been over-criticised in the past, he added, more than necessary and was a very quick driver. 'Even when he was with Alain and Ayrton he was never far behind and he's gotten better with the years,' said Jacques.

The reason he was not as consistent as Damon was the disadvantage of being a newcomer, having just 30 laps to get to know circuits on a Friday and needing most of those laps to be running near the limit to find the right settings.

There was plenty of food for thought here for Hill but he was working on positivism, intent on talking of winning and not wallowing in the despair of technical robbery in Monaco and spinning out in Barcelona's washout. He talked about team matters, acting as a leader, insisting that it would be great to have a 1–2 for himself and Jacques, a great boost for Williams, important for morale. Jacques would have massive motivation from Montreal's first sell-out 95,000 raceday crowd and would be hard to beat. He wanted to lock out the front of the grid with the blue and white cars but his personal ambition was obvious.

'I would be happy just to see the finish this weekend,' Hill said with a rueful smile. 'The last two races have been pretty miserable experiences for me. I am keen to change that. It is foremost in my mind. Getting to the finish is my goal.

'I cannot help but have higher expectations than that. Barcelona was unfortunate. I kind of got caught out by my own performance in warm-up when it was wet. The car felt good but I did not compensate enough for the colossal rain in the set-up. We made a bit of an error, I was as responsible as anyone.

'Still, I think it is very good to have 17 points [advantage] at this stage. I am going to have to slug it out with the other title contenders for the rest of the season. The history and tradition of the championship show there is always a shift in performance in the second half of the season but I feel we have the best package in our car.

'I feel I am driving better than ever. I am fitter and more refreshed than I was at the same time last year. I have all the feelings of someone who has a good situation at this point.

'I started the season with my sights set on the championship and that is still the intention. Nothing has changed but I cannot take anything for granted. Nothing will be given freely. I will have to go and fight for it.'

Someone suggested the pressure was off because Villeneuve was expected to win, had all the attention, even to the extent of complaining that he felt like a 'a mouse in a wheel' with so much public attention. Could Hill give Jacques any advice on the weekend?

'I would not presume to give him advice,' said Hill diplomatically. 'He has shown he can look after himself very well. I know he wants to do well in Canada and is keen to show his fans what he can do in F1.

'There is never a time when the pressure is off me. I put pressure on myself all the time, I want to do well in every race. The world watches and I have my fans in Britain so I want to do well for them, too.'

Canada had not seen such crowds since the 1976 Olympics and Hill, recalling the Nigel Mansell theory that he was blown along by the support at Silverstone, conceded: 'It can be a big motivation to race in front of your own crowd – you know, the Mansell factor of two seconds a lap.'

He reiterated his desire to make it to the finish, making it sound as if he might drive with a touch more caution, nursing the car to the flag for some valuable points rather than just chasing a victory.

'If I am in there fighting past halfway, and things are looking good, then I will want to win – I sure do,' explained Hill, 'but I want to score some points in the championship.'

He was aware that Schumacher was sounding more and more confident, spending huge amounts of time testing, trying new things for Ferrari, but he had a little dig at the Barcelona situation where the Italians had got it right.

'If you have a situation where you can afford to gamble, that favours you at certain times,' he said, hinting that Ferrari, struggling to find consistency, had nothing to lose by taking a risk on their set-up at the previous race. Though it had worked perfectly.

'Michael is saying this is a crunch race and that is interesting. It may indicate he has high hopes here.'

The circuit he described as tricky with a lot of time spent coming out of slow corners. Traction and horsepower would be important although this time he laid off Renault. A silly chicane inserted into the back straight to slow the cars had been removed giving another overtaking opportunity, something Formula One badly needed.

Frank Williams, sitting quietly in the back of the garage as his cars were rebuilt in preparation for Friday's practice sessions, confirmed for the first time that Hill was not yet on contract for 1997 but insisted it was just too early to talk about.

'Damon is much more mature now,' he said. 'He can undoubtedly cope better with pressure. He is stronger mentally and physically and he is equipped to take on Michael.

'It is a great season, isn't it? F1 is a tremendous sport. We have had some wonderful races and we are going to have a lot more before the end of the year. We anticipated the other teams would improve. They try hard, we work harder.

'It is like running the four-minute mile. You break it and then someone comes along and is even faster. Everyone has to really work to get faster and it is marvellous to be part of that. That is what makes it so good as we all compete to be the best.'

That night Hill and Villeneuve went off to a massive Rothmans public party where for $10 a time, fans could see, hear and possibly question their heroes. On stage was a group called 'The Untouchables' but the name fitted the drivers better than anyone in this year's championship.

Gazza Inspires

Hill certainly underlined that fact on a hazy, warm Friday morning when he was fastest but for the first time was revealed the new Ferrari high 'shark' nose which had been tested, originally rejected by Schumacher and then accepted when he found it was worth two-tenths of a second a lap. The difference between success and failure in F1 is hairline.

The afternoon session provided a few thrills with the Benettons battling it out for first and second, Jean Alesi winning before spinning right at the end while Gerhard Berger kissed a corner at speed. Others were spinning and twitching, adjusting front wings, trying new tyres, changing dampers. Hill was a satisfied fourth.

On Saturday morning, Villeneuve, who had mused that the shorter Ferrari would twist through the corners quicker than the Williams, gave the early risers something to cheer when he was fastest in the warm-up. Alesi had another excursion up an escape road and Eddie Irvine switched to the high nose on his Ferrari. As if to confirm Hill's own fears Irvine said: 'I would not like to be in his shoes at the moment. Damon is at a tricky stage of the season and things are going Michael's way right now.'

Qualifying was another exciting hour, twice red-flagged as first Alesi, in his third moment on the track, spun and destroyed a tyre wall, damaging his Benetton. To ease his discomfort, team-mate Berger emulated the feat later. It finished with Hill taking his fifth pole of the season, disappointing the packed crowd who saw him take the front position of the local hero by just two-hundreths of a second while Schumacher was just over one-tenth behind. It was fiercely close and the top eight were within a second of Hill.

Villeneuve was just as annoyed as his fans for he felt that he had erred. 'The car was quicker than the lap time we got. On fresh tyres I was too cautious in braking areas. I found I was braking too early and slowing down too much.'

His uncle Jacques and his father's former manager had both criticised him for not showing enough respect to Gilles' name but he refused to get involved in the media debate.

Hill was in fine form. Admitting that he had not done a good job in Spain, he was determined to make up for that. 'It was a real cliffhanger out there,' he said. 'I really had to get my head down to beat Jacques' time.

'He was very fast on his first run and I could not beat his time, so I had to do a bit of thinking. I talked to the engineers and we made a couple of changes for the second run but I really had to work hard. It is going to be a tough race. Reliability and tactics will be a factor.'

Schumacher was not as happy and insisted that the new nose on the car was not some sort of wonder – not a 'Copperfield' as he put it, referring to David Copperfield, the illusionist.

That morning, England had beaten Scotland in a thrilling Euro 96 match and Hill was quick to seek me out in the audience to say with a smile: 'How did the football go?" He knew for during the red flag time, the lads in the factory in Britain had fed TV pictures down the line to the pits.

'Can I say congratulations to Paul Gascoigne [scorer of a brilliant goal for England]. I could see his goal and it was quite something. We beat Scotland 2–0, you know.'

It was good banter and there was more to come, for BBC motorsport commentator, Murray Walker, had been awarded the OBE and when Hill met up with him, he dropped to one knee in front of The Voice to offer his congratulations.

Mean Streak

Yet again, Hill pipped Villeneuve to fastest time in the Sunday morning warm-up. It seemed like an omen that Hill was always able just to get his nose in front . . . and it proved right when the race erupted into action.

Disaster had already struck for Schumacher who was left stranded as Hill led the cars off on their parade lap. The Ferrari had fuel pressure problems and the mechanics worked in a frenzy to get the engine fired up. He started from the back of the field with a heavy fuel load and already his chance had gone.

Hill made no mistake at the start, showing a mean streak as he went into the first corner with Villeneuve right behind. The duel was deadly in the afternoon sun but after only 10 seconds, Hill had the race firmly in his grasp.

Hill had heard on the radio of Schumacher's problems and that added to the import of the initial fight for both men believed that whoever got into the first corner ahead would probably win and they sat on the grid gripped with the realisation that it was now or never. Hill seized the moment but later Villeneuve, while not complaining, made it clear that he was a touch surprised at his team-mate's move.

Hill had decided on a two-stop strategy, going faster with a lighter load which would put less strain on brakes and tyres. Villeneuve went with the more traditional one-stop and that put him at a further disadvantage on the run to the first corner but he was fired up. They both knew the situation.

'We sit at the same briefing so we know what we are doing,' said Hill. 'I felt I had to do something because there was little more than a cigarette paper between us all weekend. It was vital that I stayed ahead at the start. After that it went smoothly.'

Those who considered him too gentlemanly on the track were surprised to see Hill bare his teeth and Villeneuve admitted: 'My start was good, a little bit better than Damon's. I am sure Damon was looking hard in his mirrors because he went right, then left, so I had to go across the track twice, and he was inside for the first turn. It was a bit more than I might have expected but I have no complaints.'

One hour and 36 minutes later, that start saw Hill celebrate the halfway mark of the season with a crucial win which silenced the crowd, the critics and his own inner doubts. No one consulted Villeneuve but most agreed when Schumacher put extra fizz in Hill's champagne by declaring: 'Maybe the championship is already Damon's.'

Some 95,000 had squeezed in to see Villeneuve celebrate Father's Day and the possibility of emotional overload was huge until near the end as the French-Canadian chased hard to make their dreams come true. If not quite silent, the crowd was polite as Hill rejoiced after taking his lead back to 21 points over Villeneuve.

111

There was cause for an extra smile, too, if he wanted to enjoy the pains of another, for Schumacher and Ferrari had had a spectacularly embarrassing day while the Williams cars went round without a cough. Schumacher had lived up to his reputation, carving his way through the field to reach seventh place by the 41st lap when he came in for a refuelling stop. As he set off along the pit lane again, only one rear tyre seemed to be touching the ground and seconds later one of the driveshafts fell off the car onto the track.

A Forti mechanic picked it up as Schumacher headed out, pulling in at the end to retire the Ferrari. That completed an abysmal day for the famed team; Eddie Irvine had already pulled over as he chased round in the leading group on lap 2. The car picked up pace again but Irvine dumped it in the garage at the end of the lap with a broken right push-rod.

Hill halted on the 27th lap and Villeneuve, to the delight of the home crowd, led until he made his only stop on lap 36. Hill took over at the front again and opened up a lead of 29 seconds which was enough to get him back on the track with 13 seconds of a cushion after his second stop on lap 49. Villeneuve set the fastest lap of the race two laps from the end but it came too late.

'I was really pushing to make sure Damon had to push as well,' said Villeneuve. 'The strategy depended a lot on the start and on the backmarkers. I got held up behind Johnny Herbert which cost me time, otherwise it could have been a lot closer.'

Only eight cars finished the race but it was fitting that Martin Brundle should come sixth to score a single point for it was his 150th F1 start and the highly popular driver from King's Lynn was due some good luck after a miserable time adjusting to the Jordan car. When he began racing in 1984, cars operated without fuel stops, dragging 230 litres on board from the start compared with 140 now. Drivers can no longer blame something in the car for a spin or slowness, for the telemetry reveals as much as a team wants about the performance of the car, every movement of the clutch or accelerator, every jolt in the suspension.

'We're all working too hard now,' said Brundle whose difficult season had given rise to rumours that he would retire at the end of the season or even be replaced for the last few races. 'There is not so much time to have fun. The pressure is almost too much.'

Interestingly, he preferred the current crop of drivers more than at any other time of his career, thanking the 1994 reconstitution of the Grand Prix Drivers Association, as one reason for their friendliness. Names like Rosberg, Mansell, Prost, Lauda, Piquet, Senna – 'They were all very, very strong characters,' said Brundle, 'and there was perhaps a tension and lack of friendliness that are much less apparent today.'

Hill, an amiable man most of the time, was certainly full of bonhomie as he bid adieu to Montreal for he was much relieved to have his eighteenth win. Alesi had been a remote third as the Benettons struggled again and the two McLarens, although fourth with Coulthard and fifth for Hakkinen, had been distant objects.

'I had two races without a win and no matter what anyone says, you do start to worry about these things. Now I can head for France feeling a lot better than I did when I left Spain.

'To win the championship we need to push really hard in the next five races and France, Britain and Germany are particularly crucial. There is a long way to go and the title is not won. I know Michael has said that the title looks likely for me but I expect he will continue to show up at races. I don't think we have seen the last of him. We are only halfway through and there will be a lot more challenges yet.'

Frank Williams, smiling at a 50-point lead for his team over Ferrari in the world constructors' championship, laughed when he heard that Schumacher had abdicated for Hill. 'He would be dangerous if he were driving a pram,' he joked.

Schumacher had even gone as far as saying that Hill deserved the title for the way he had driven. 'He is 27 points ahead of me and he could finish second six times with me winning those races and still be champion,' said the man with the golden touch.

113

'I have always said that the title was out of my reach in the first year with Ferrari. They had fourteen retirements last season and you cannot expect to sort that out in twelve months. We will get better and more reliable but it will not be enough this season.'

Schumacher rarely gets it wrong, and if he tipped Hill for the title, that was good enough for many who headed for the bookies to throw money on the man who would be king.

Race 8: Canadian Grand Prix

Result	Drivers (overall)	Constructors (overall)
1. Damon Hill (GB)	1. Hill 53	1. Williams 85
2. Jacques Villeneuve (Can)	2. Villeneuve 32	2. Ferrari 35
3. Jean Alesi (Fra)	3. Schumacher 26	3. Benetton 28
4. David Coulthard (GB)		
5. Mika Hakkinen (Fin)		
6. Martin Brundle (GB)		

10

Advantage Hill

Damon Hill warmed up for the Grands Prix in France and Britain by going testing at Silverstone and by getting a tennis lesson from Wimbledon champion Pete Sampras. Sampras, a big fan of Formula One, had expressed interest in watching Grand Prix cars as he spent time in Britain before defending his title, and was a guest at the three-day test.

He felt Hill was underrated, Hill agreed and they exchanged a helmet for a racket, set up a little court outside the pit lane garage and had a gentle knock-about. Hill suggested Sampras work on the backhand, Sampras advised less understeer and good fun was had by all.

The smiles faltered a little, however, during the test when France provided one of the great Formula One shocks of the season even before the teams reached Magny-Cours as Renault, providers of power for Williams and Benetton, decided to quit at the end of their contracts in 1997. Rumours had rolled around for months but the car company finally came clean after six weeks of debate within the firm about future costs and commitments.

The teams expressed their disappointment at the decision and Damon Hill arrived at the circuit and admitted: 'I am footloose and fancy free at the end of the season and this could have a bearing on my future.'

It was almost the first time that talk of the expiration of his contract at the end of the season had arisen but he glossed over the issue, declaring regret at the move but insisting that his whole focus was on winning this year's championship and the French Grand Prix in particular.

Speculation was rife as to how the teams would sort out the power vacuum in 1998. Already Honda had hinted strongly that they would return to F1 in 1998 after five years out. Peugeot, expected by many to recruit much of their national rival's expertise after the pull-out, were contracted to Jordan until the end of 1997. Ford was commited to a five-year deal for its factory engines with Jackie Stewart's new team which was scheduled to launch in 1997 and Mercedes were locked into a six-year deal with McLaren and had no wish to supply two teams. BMW were said to be looking closely at returning but the scramble was on for real power.

Renault's decision was unexpected because they had been so successful, the dominant manufacturer with 49 wins with Williams and 10 with Benetton since returning to the sport in 1989 after a break. Having helped Williams win the drivers' championship with Nigel Mansell in 1992, Alain Prost a year later, plus two constructors' championships, they had done a co-deal with Benetton.

Michael Schumacher won the drivers' title, the team took the constructors' but Patrick Faure, the Renault Sport managing director, said: 'We have not lost money for nine years but we can't forget that F1 costs money. What we are saying is that the value for money is not as interesting as it once was.'

The Elf fuel company had also decided to depart from Grand Prix racing but a significant entrant to the sport had shown up at Silverstone when Bridgestone tyres tested with Arrows, threatening Goodyear's long-standing F1 monopoly.

Hill arrived still coming to terms with the novelty of being third in a test session at Silverstone, especially as the fastest man had been Williams' test driver, Jean-Christophe Boullion. Hill had been trying out an improved Renault engine and trying set-ups for the forthcoming British Grand Prix. He also arrived the day after England had lost on penalties to Germany in the semi-finals of Euro 96. Are you the man to carry Britain's sporting colours this weekend for a rare summer sporting victory, he was asked, tongue-in-cheek. He laughed but he was as disappointed as anyone around the table. 'It was sad. I watched at home in Ireland and it was really exciting, edge of the seat stuff. They did a bloody good job. I did not have any nails left at the end.

'Sad news about Renault and Elf, too. They won't ease off, I am sure. They are here for 1997 and I certainly believe they will continue to put everything into it. There is pride at stake for Renault who will want to be as effective as they can be.

'There are another twenty-four Grands Prix left and they will want to win those and set new standards before they move on.'

His concern again was that the opposition was closing in although the finish of the Canadian race indicated otherwise, with Ferrari faces as red as the cars, McLaren reliable but plodding and Benetton still a long way short of their previous season's form.

'The next eight races will be much tougher than the first eight,' he said. 'I think it will be really tough. We clearly had an advantage in the early races but not so much now.'

In his head he fought a vigilant battle to stay alert, not to be complacent but at times the facts did not bear witness to the words, yet he was to be proved right about Villeneuve.

'He will be running quicker for the rest of the year. He knows some of the circuits better, he knows F1 better and he is still in with a very strong chance of challenging me for the title. There is no complacency on my part and there is no feeling that the job is anywhere near being finished. I have prepared myself for the last half of the season. I am proud to have won eighteen races for Renault – more than anyone else. I was surprised to hear that. I look forward to more.'

His forecast that Ferrari would improve did not quite put him in the Mystic Meg category but who could have predicted that the Italians would continue to be as desperate for so long.

Hill expected much from his car now and was satisfied that the team was pressing ahead after Canada, putting some things in the pipeline to make the car quicker. Magny-Cours is a circuit where power counted although the mix of engine and aero-dynamics package and chassis would come more into play.

'I am confident we can do well. Win? Yes. The challenge may be stronger from Benetton and maybe McLaren but I would be very disappointed if I were not, as a team, looking at winning here.

'I have not thought about contracts or anything like that. My thoughts are purely on the championship. I have a lead which I want to extend if I can and it is vital for me to keep the ball rolling and to keep scoring points. I will have to race for it. I don't expect it to land in my lap. My confidence is high and I am enjoying my driving. Canada was good in that it was a great boost to my confidence.

'I mean all the races are vital. You cannot single out one but if you have two non-finishes as I had, the burden gets a little heavier.

'Complacency is the great threat. I could not finish the next two races and still lead by one point so that would make it a little more exciting – for you and for me – but it is not what I want to happen.

'It would be a big mistake for me to believe that all I had to do was soft-pedal for the rest of the season. For sure my lead would drastically diminish and vanish, evaporate and before I knew it, I would be going into the last three races with a very small margin. I have to attack these races with the same mental approach as I effected in previous races.'

He was challenged about the championship. Why not just accept it was almost in the bag, the rest of the teams were on F1's backroads while the Williams car was on the motorway?

'No, it's not in the bank,' he said earnestly. 'You see, it is paper money. It is non-existent. A 21-point lead in the championship at this stage is not something you can take away with you. It doesn't really exist. The only result that exists is when the championship is decided.'

So had he amused himself by working out where he could win the title?

'That would be a big mistake,' he fired back. 'Doing those mental calculations are amusing and time-filling but if I could predict the future I would make a lot of money. I know from my own experience that you cannot plan things happening the way you want. You just have to do the best you can. I have to ensure it goes the way I want it to.'

Jacques' Crash

Hill had had three pole positions at Magny-Cours, a circuit he liked, but had not won and he appeared to be talking himself up again. Interestingly, Villeneuve did not appreciate the 2.67 mile circuit, commenting: 'I don't like it as it is a very modern type of track with no straight lines and corners everywhere.'

Yet it was Hill who careered off the circuit in the first practice session, the car clipping a kerb and bucking and rearing like a wild horse as it leapt across a gravel trap. He emerged from a cloud of dust with a dented car but his confidence was intact.

'I had a pretty bad start, went over the chicane and had a bit of a moment as I got airborne,' he said, 'but it is not too bad. We made some progress and we are heading in the right direction.'

Villeneuve was seventh as he tried different set-ups and for the first time both men would use the new evolution of the Renault RS8B engine, a more powerful and versatile unit.

Hakkinen in the McLaren was fastest, with the local team, Ligier, on their home track, looking good as Olivier Panis went second. Yet Martin Brundle, the Jordan driver, reported: 'Take my word for it, the Williams cars are flying. Just wait until they are in race trim. They are trying things but they are a class apart.'

In fact, they were struggling to find the right touch and in qualifying, it was Michael Schumacher who was surprised to get the thirteenth pole position of his career, while Hill finished second and Villeneuve was lucky to walk away from a big shunt. The French-Canadian, who ran wide coming out of the high-speed Estoril corner, slammed into the tyre wall, ripped off two wheels and bounced back onto the track where David Coulthard just missed the Williams as he arrived on the scene.

Villeneuve needed physio after the session but he had qualified sixth.

Hill was disappointed for he had been quicker on split times in the first sector but lost it on the second and when it was pointed out, he exclaimed: 'We are aware of that. I lost it all on the quick chicane on the return leg where I had a moment and lost all the time. I would have had pole but for that. It was a driver error, I'm afraid.

'I have had three pole positions here in the last three years and I haven't got it this time. Perhaps that means my luck will change.'

The new engine, he said, was 'not a quantum leap' but offered a small improvement in mid-range which made response better and stronger where it was needed.

Ferrari's Black Day

The Sunday morning stroll round the track is normally as uneventful as a Ron Dennis press conference at McLaren, but this one turned into a rodeo. Villeneuve, recovering fast, was quickest but Hill found himself in what he labelled 'the warm-up from hell'. He collided with Heinz-Harald Frentzen at the hairpin, ripping off a wheel of the Sauber, not seeing the German bearing down on him because he was fiddling with something in the cockpit – but at least Hill had the decency to go and apologise for his lapse. Hill took out the spare car but a brake problem then saw him go straight on and through the sand trap.

Schumacher also slid off after locking the brakes and many were the slips and slides but there was extra drama, for Eddie Irvine's Ferrari was found on the official inspection to have illegally big aerodynamic deflectors. The Ferrari garage doors were slammed down as many moved in and Jean Todt, their sporting director, had a lively exchange with Williams' technical director Patrick Head. The suspicion was that the other two Ferraris might be illegal but they were cleared and Irvine,

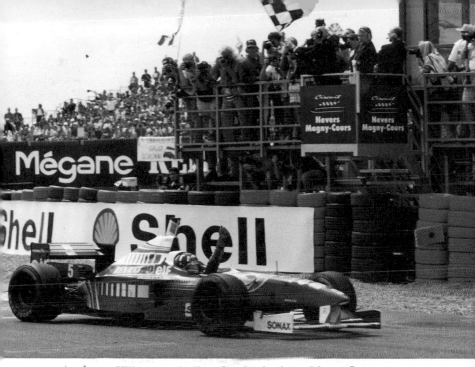

A French salute ... Hill crosses the line after dominating at Magny-Cours.

Defending Wimbledon champion Pete Sampras gives Hill a few words of advice – but then lost his own title.

Final instructions in the garage at Silverstone from technical director Patrick Head.

Hill leads from the start to delight the home crowds but crashed out soon after.

The long walk home comes to an end in the pits as Hill discusses his accident with Frank Williams.

'Have you been sacked?' was the main question when Hill met the media in Germany.

Williams' chief designer Adrian Newey offers advice to Hill – but he got it wrong with a bad mistake in Belgium.

No hard feelings between Hill and Heinz-Harald Frentzen when they meet up after the German driver was hired to replace Damon in the Williams team for 1997.

The strain shows in Italy.
Hill failed to clinch the title
in the last four European
races. (*Fmpics*)

Murray Walker is given a farewell tribute for his BBC efforts by Hill and (*from left*)
David Coulthard, Martin Brundle and Johnny Herbert.

Hill is caught by Villeneuve who outpaced his title rival in Portugal.

Delight and despair in Estoril: a triumphant Villeneuve savours victory while Hill
leaves him to it.

Toasting a new deal for next year with the Arrows team and his new boss Tom Walkinshaw. The championship champagne was still on ice.

Glory at last for Hill as he takes the title in Japan to emulate his father Graham, twice world champion in the 1960s. (*Empics*)

having qualified tenth, was relegated to the back of the grid.

Ferraris at the front and back – but not for long. Having just managed to get on the grid in Canada, Schumacher now suffered the ultimate embarrassment of not reaching the grid. Hill tried very, very hard to keep the smile off his face but just as suddenly as the vast cloud of smoke and oil had erupted from Schumacher's engine, his smile lit up the room. By then, the world champion had departed, leaving from Nevers in his private jet to escape the agony of Ferrari.

Hill's resistance had lasted longer than the Ferrari's but then that managed only 20 seconds before it blew up in front of the Englishman's startled gaze on the parade lap even before the start. Suddenly Hill could not see the hairpin, the day had turned dark; while for him it was temporary, for Schumacher it was another black day. He fought the temptation to believe that, even in that moment, he had won the French Grand Prix. But the collective groan of 80,000 spectators, which rose into the sky with the smoke, proved that they thought otherwise.

It was not that they did not want Hill to win, although many did, it was more that they knew they had been robbed of a great motor-race. Schumacher was still walking back to the pits as Hill passed, off the lights, on his way to the nineteenth win of his career, driving with relentless efficiency to the delight of the thousands of Union Jack-waving supporters who had travelled to central France.

Slowly but surely Damon's Divisions had built up: they may not be Schumacher's army, but how they made themselves heard as Hill crushed his rival's avowed intention of a German 1–2 in the Euro 96 final and in Formula One. That lost something in the translation for the 1–2 was provided by Hill and Villeneuve, who finished second, unless you count the Ferrari double of Schumacher out and then Irvine after five laps with gearbox trouble.

'It is never a good idea to enjoy someone else's misfortune,' said Hill, remembering a few of his own. 'I was a little worried that his engine was going to blow in a really big way and leave huge oil slicks so I backed off. When it did go after the initial smoke, it went in a proper way, dumping a lot of oil which sprayed over my visor and the front of the car and the track, leaving a line.'

But what exactly had been his feelings at the moment he knew red car number one was out? At last, Hill cracked and so did his face. 'I was amazed, stunned – but delighted,' he said with a grin.

'It clearly changed my thinking about the race. But I still had to make a good start because it is easy to get distracted by something like that. Afer that everything went perfectly for me.'

Schumacher tried to be diplomatic. 'At first I was very angry as I saw all the team's hard work disappear but then I calmed down,' he said. 'It is usless to panic.' He even tried some humour. 'I saw a big cloud behind but I did not know if it was smoke or rain.'

Todt described it as the blackest day of his career while Renault were overjoyed to dominate their home race. As Hill had walked back to the motor home after the race, an engineer from another team remarked: 'There is a God and he is not Italian', reflecting the technical feeling in the pits that Ferrari had been lucky not to be further penalised for their aerodynamic mix-up. Johnny Herbert fell foul of the same rule, finishing eleventh only to be disqualified.

Ironically, a few days after announcing their exit from F1, Renault delighted the whole of France for the Benettons had done well, Alesi third, Berger fourth and that gave the engine manufacturer a magnificent 1–2–3–4. Just to complete a day of doubles, McLaren had taken fifth with Hakkinen and sixth for Coulthard.

A great result for Hill who had managed to bore the crowd with sensible, dominating but safe driving which gave him the fastest lap, too. Hill now had a 25-point lead going to the British Grand Prix but still would not believe publicly that his name would end up on the drivers' trophy.

Ferrari were under pressure with Todt offering to resign as comments such as 'The Ferrari reputation has gone up in smoke' and 'Ferrari are skidding to ridicule' appeared. His opposite number at Williams, Head, promised more improvements in the car for Silverstone and Germany, two high-speed circuits.

Head was losing his caution and said: 'I think it would be very difficult for someone to get back at us very strongly this year. We have some special bits to come. We have a good engine, car and driver package. Damon is very focused.'

Alain Prost, who had driven with Damon in the Williams team in 1993 when he won the last of his four world titles, was also impressed.

'The media seems to support Schumacher more so it is difficult for Damon,' he said. 'If one guy captures the ear of the media, then you are screwed. You can lose 20 per cent of your potential and I think Damon is vulnerable to that.

'You can imagine what would have happened if Damon had done what Michael did on the opening lap at Monaco. Can you imagine what the press would have said? I think Damon is much more concentrated on his job than he has been in previous races, much better than last year.'

It was the highest compliment from the little Frenchman. All Damon had to do was turn up at Silverstone to win and put the jewel in the world crown. How little we knew.

Race 9: French Grand Prix

Result	Drivers (overall)	Constructors (overall)
1. Damon Hill (GB)	1. Hill 63	1. Williams 101
2. Jacques Villeneuve (Can)	2. Villeneuve 38	2=Ferrari 35
3. Jean Alesi (Fra)	3. Schumacher 26	2=Benetton 35
4. Gerhard Berger (Aut)		
5. Mika Hakkinen (Fin)		
6. David Coulthard (GB)		

11

Copse Corners Hill

British Grand Prix, Silverstone: 14 July

Hill had a price on his head by the time he set up camp at Silverstone for now there was more interest in his contract and the fact that Williams did not have their top man even on an option. He was, it was reported, looking for an increase from around £4.5 million a year to £10 million as world champion. Still considerably less than Schumacher's basic of £16 million a season but far more than Frank Williams had paid to anyone apart from Ayrton Senna. Hill would not talk money, not wanting to be seen in the public eye as someone with more interest in the bank balance than his points tally before his home race as he went for the world title.

'I would dearly like to win the world championship,' he said. 'If I can, then I would like nothing better than to stay with the Rothmans Williams Renault team ... but I want to race next year in the most competitive package I can.

'I don't doubt that they will be competitive but I still wonder, because Renault are going to quit at the end of next year, how much momentum will they be able to keep up next season.'

His status had risen considerably since his sour crash with Schumacher a year earlier as their duel reached another destructive episode. Now Hill was clear leader of the championship, with the best strike rate on the grid. Hill had overtaken Schumacher as the most successful current driver going by the statistics with 40 points-scoring races from 60 events giving him a 66.66 per cent rate.

Schumacher, of course, after two world titles, had settled for figures to impress his bank manager in the Swiss vaults.

Hill had now become the fourth most successful British driver behind Nigel Mansell, Jackie Stewart and Jim Clark. A British victory would put him level with Schumacher's twenty career wins but the German could not resist breaking his self-imposed truce in his back-biting to say: 'He may win as many races, but I have two world championships.'

Hill laughed it off and joked about his life as a superstar, pointing to a lovely family photograph in the *Daily Express* which showed him playing guitar to say: 'I was actually singing about the leaking roof we had in the house and how I needed to get it fixed.'

It is part of his charm, part of his problem, that he was seen as a safe, dependable, family man but the real, more human side did not get across. There was no Mansell or Senna-type hysteria around Hill, just an appreciation which seemed to puzzle the public at times. He had several times stated that he did not want to get involved in the Grand Prix bullshit but in 1995 he was drawn into it, but never enough to put his side as vigorously or as cutely as Schumacher. Know the rules, play the game and you can win. Clean conscience was great but clean-up was what Schumacher had done.

Now Hill was comfortable with his place in the sport. He was his own man but he would not analyse why things had changed, as if fearing to tempt the fates and raise old ghosts.

He worried more about taking his children to Chessington Zoo, as he had before Silverstone. He knew he might have a hard time from autograph hunters but he said: 'I am determined the children will not miss out because of me. A few people did approach me but I just pointed out I was with the family and it was fine.'

Hill had worked harder at being a personality rather than a dour figure on the podium or in the pits and it did seem to have a beneficial effect all round. 'This season I have been able to just be myself more, certainly until now, and I want that to continue. I started the season determined to show people who I am. At the race track I can be serious but I am not like that all the time. It is all part of Formula One but so much of what is talked and written about is conjecture, guesswork. I like to do what I am good at, driving, and forget about the wind-up factor.'

He denied that he took any gloating pleasure from the struggles of rival Michael Schumacher. 'Contrary to what people think, I do not spend my life thinking about Schumacher,' he said.

'I tend to spend 99 per cent of my time thinking about Damon Hill and how he is going to do in the world championship. It is not about Hill v. Schumacher. It never has been for me. It is Hill versus Hill.

'I think I have an extremely tough mental make-up. That has never been different. What has changed is that I decided to turn my back on anything that was not relevant to winning the championship. I am better organised, with people dealing with the demands of being in the limelight or the forefront of F1. They give me good advice. I had a steep learning curve and I have been trying to get up to speed with everything. I am not the kind of person who rushes into things. I am cautious by nature.

'I don't rush out and buy a jet or spend like it is going out of fashion to keep up with the big boys. I try to keep a real position. If you are not careful, F1 can go to your head.'

Yet Hill was one of the big boys and a win at Silverstone would project him even further. With Georgie, his wife, sons Oliver and Joshua and baby Tabitha, he had settled nicely in Dublin and now had the use of a private plane to help him move around Europe quickly. Not that he had bought it, as Schumacher had done, it was simply rented.

But would he want his own children to go motor-racing? 'It is dangerous but very enjoyable,' he said after a moment's consideration. 'I have been testing in the rain and it is great fun, sliding the car around. I do love being in the car.

'Frightening? That is not the right word. The adrenaline goes up but I would say that makes you very awake. It is like my dad. You could not get him out of the car. He was 45 when he stopped.'

It was reported that Damon had told Georgie that he would stop in 2000 but he laughs when asked about it and says: 'It sounds a good round figure. I will be 40 then – but it depends when you are talking about. That won't be until the September. And it might be a good season.'

He wanted to do something special for the fans at Silverstone. Maybe a win that was as dominant as, say, France. It would be special to do something like that in front of a British crowd.

In the British Racing Drivers Club house at Silverstone, they presented Hill with the Mike Hawthorn Memorial Trophy for the third year running. The trophy is given to the British or Commonwealth driver who has scored the most points in the Formula One championship. Only Jacques Villeneuve had a chance of preventing him winning it four years in succession.

Even as he accepted the trophy, Hill's mind drifted back to the warm days as a little boy who used the paddock as his playground. From his time as a toddler, as he watched and waited for his father, to now as the man who takes on the mantle of the latest Great British Hope of the sporting summer, Hill bridges the gap with ease.

In a brief escape from the present, Hill could see himself thirty years ago when the roars and applause were for the legends of the 1960s. 'My impressions were usually of the pits. I remember my mother working in the pits, keeping the lap chart for my father.

'I was looked after by various au-pairs and other wives of people in the sport, in the doghouse, which used to be a big wooden hut near the start line. We never got out on the circuit. I used to play around in the paddock. It was more like a playground when I first came here.

'Now I am here with people cheering for me and hoping I will win. I have had that extreme pleasure once before. There is nothing quite like it for any sportsman who wins in front of his home crowd.'

Already the banners of support were everywhere proclaiming: Demon Damon, Hill Climb to Glory, Deadly Damon, Hill's a Hero.

'I feel I have been passed the ball a bit,' he said with a smile when asked if he could make up disappointments in tennis, golf, football and cricket. 'I have been very successful so far this year but historically the odds are against me continuing to keep up that ratio of wins for the season.

'The job is going to become more difficult. I am not trying to escape my responsibility for I do feel I have the opportunity to produce a British victory this weekend. I feel the same as anyone about British sport. We desperately want something to cheer about. I sat through the football, cricket and tennis and you can rest assured that I will be trying damn hard to give people something to cheer about on Sunday.'

Was it more difficult to drive faster as a family man with three children, asked a German reporter.

'Well, my middle son keeps telling me to keep both hands on the wheel,' said Hill. 'They look after me. The answer may be that in another way I feel more motivated to perform and drive more professionally as a father than I did before.

'If you look back, you will find that many successful drivers were fathers – my own dad, Nigel Mansell, Jackie Stewart, Alain Prost, Niki Lauda among them. Enzo Ferrari once said that drivers with children would be a second slower. If that is so, I must be driving well below my potential.'

He was relaxed and enjoying himself. His mobile phone rang as he answered questions in front of an army of television crews, radio and newspaper reporters. 'That was Bernie Ecclestone,' he joked.

How had he enjoyed doing his Pizza Hut television commercials with Murray Walker, asked someone. 'I was going to award two free pizza meals for the most original question,' he replied. 'You've just won.'

Hill was having fun again in his old playground where he was the little kid under his father's feet. Now the crowds would happily applaud him as he turned the paddock into a playground again on Sunday night.

At a different ceremony, Formula One supremo, Bernie Ecclestone, was presented with a BRDC Gold Medal, the first recipient of the new award for services to motor-racing. That was some solace for Bernie who, a week earlier, had been mugged in Knightsbridge as he and his wife, Slavica, made their way home after a night out. Three men grabbed the couple and Ecclestone was punched and kicked in the face. He suffered a broken rib and facial bruising, as the muggers took valuables including a ring said to be worth £660,000.

Serious Threat

Autograph hunters rather than muggers, although they would have done well, too, had a great time as usual at the Grand Prix for the lure of the F1 circus brought out all manner of well-known faces. Nick Faldo, the US Masters champion, was there as a guest of the Rothmans Williams team, Tony Blair, the Labour leader, Kenneth Clarke, the suede-shoe-clad Chancellor of the Exchequer, England rugby players Victor Ubogu and Will Carling, ice dancers Torvill and Dean, former world motorcycle champions Kevin Schwantz, Jim Redman and Carl Fogarty.

A dull, cloudy Friday saw the usual traffic jams outside Silverstone and now the teams could find out if their work had all been in vain. Gary Anderson of Jordan explained how they prepared by looking at the basic format of the circuit, taking into account the nature of the corners, and then running a lap simulation on the computer.

'We feed in the parameters of the car, amount of downforce, weight of car and tyre compound among other details and the computer can predict a lap time. We can then change the data, less downforce maybe, and see if it gives us a quicker time or not.

'There are four basic areas to take into account when setting up a racing car: aerodynamics, mechanics, transmission and engine. The aerodynamic package consists of wings and ride heights. The mechanical package would include shock absorber settings, springs, roll bars, dampers and cambers. The transmission is gear ratios and the differential and then there is the engine set-up which is looked after by Peugeot.

'A quick car is a balanced car even if that sometimes means compromising the grip at the front or rear. At Silverstone it is difficult for the circuit has fast, sweeping bends but it also has a very slow, tight infield section. Top speed at Silverstone is 185 mph, not as fast as you would think. It is also a very exposed circuit because it is so flat and that means you have to take into account the wind.

'Although it varies from team to team, I would say it is about 80 per cent down to the engineer to set up the car. The remaining 20 per cent is very important, for at the end of the day the driver is the one charged with extracting a time from the car. If he feels confident in the car, he will be able to dig deeper inside himself to produce that all-important lap time.'

Hill talked us through his lap, describing Silverstone as one of the greatest circuits we go to, with a challenging combination of high-speed and slow corners, long straights and a wide track.

'The first corner is about a 195 kph in third gear, a light dab on the brake and down to third from sixth gear. After that you are up to sixth again into the best part of the circuit, which is the Becketts section, a very fast right hand followed by a slower left-hand bend and then an even slower right-hander.

'We enter in sixth and drop down the gears to fifth, fourth and maybe even third. Then you come out of the last part of Becketts having pulled four G right, then four G left, then four G right again before accelerating out onto the Hangar Straight at 160 kph. We brake heavily into the new Stowe Corner, which is an improvement over the last Stowe, which was too slow – it was just a stop, turn right and accelerate – but this one has a much faster entry, although it does have some bumps in it which makes it quite difficult.

'If I come down the Hangar Straight and get a good tow off somebody, then it would be possible to go up the inside in Stowe because the line requires us to stay left, so it is possible for someone to slip up inside if they are good. That is a fourth gear corner, where we are doing 160 kph on the apex of the corner.

'Then I go down into Vale, braking for one of the slowest corners of the circuit, Club, which we take in first gear. It is very bumpy. I have to use a little bit of kerb there and it is very diffcult to accelerate because of the bumps, and then accelerating round Club Corner, up through second, third, just getting fourth on the exit, fifth and then up to sixth just before Abbey Corner.

'This is quite a tricky left-hander. It is very difficult to see the apex of the corner as it's over the crest of the hill, and the car is always sliding there as generally the wind is behind – it actually points exactly south-west – so if there is a sou-wester I always have oversteer into Abbey Curve.

'I accelerate and try to stay on the power round the right-hand kink, which is taken in third gear, through Bridge Corner, which is almost flat out in fifth. This is still as challenging as it ever was, high G, high loading, quite bumpy corner. Then I come racing through there into Priory, which is quite a big stop, and down into second gear and first for Brooklands, which is the slowest corner on the circuit.

'Then we have to manage with the slow speed section of the circuit and the bumps in the two Luffield corners and the Woodcote Corner. It is very important to get this one right, as it leads into the final straight. I should be at my maximum speed across the start–finish line to get a quick lap off to a good start, so the last corner is also the first one to get right when qualifying.'

At last the Friday session got going and 33,000 spectators were there to see the free practice. For most of the day, Hill was top man, fastest in the morning despite feeling that further circuit improvements had left the surface slippery.

'We will get better tomorrow,' he said, 'but I can't really say that I have worked out the best chassis set-up yet.'

In the final minutes of the afternoon session, Villeneuve switched to a fresh set of tyres for his final run after picking up a puncture and the change took him round the 3.1 mile circuit in 1 minute 27.541 seconds, seven-tenths of a second faster than Hill, at an average speed of around 130 mph.

That put him top with his team-mate second and Hill responded with a smile, admitting: 'Jacques looks very impressive. He has put down a marker and he is very intent on a good result. He is obviously fired up and is a serious threat – my main challenger by the looks of it. I will have to squeeze everything out of myself to beat him.'

Villeneuve, for his part, looked confident, pleased to have put a shot across Hill's bow, and said: 'I will be giving it my best shot. Damon won my home race and it would be nice to reverse that. It is looking good at the moment.'

Such were Ferrari's problems that Luca de Montezemolo, the president, and former Fiat empire chairman, Gianni Agnelli, had flown to Britain to look at the preparations. Now there was more talk about Hill's contract for 19.7, or the lack of it.

Was it possible that Hill, who had been in touch with Ferrari the year before, would be an attractive proposition for them, especially as Eddie Irvine's contract was up at the end of the year?

'Hill is a very good driver but for Ferrari it is not our idea to have two number one drivers in the team and for this reason I do not think we would be interested in him,' said Montezemolo.

Damon was looking for a new contract with Williams but also a massive hike on his £4.5 million-a-year deal, a story which appeared in most newspapers that week. Frank Williams, as always, would not be drawn but said: 'I got a lot of press cuttings on my desk, all saying the same thing and I thought that Damon was sending me a message.

'But the press cuttings fell off the desk into the the rubbish bin, as they always do. No doubt I will be talking to Damon very soon. Clearly he is highly regarded not only inside our team but also outside. I can make no comment whether he will or will not be with us next year. I simply don't know.'

That was to be a significant comment in the light of subsequent events in September. Ironically, it was Villeneuve who was being asked if it was true that he might not serve out the second year of his contract but would be replaced by Heinz-Harald Frentzen.

'I know where I stand and that is all that counts,' said Villeneuve. 'All it takes is one person in the paddock to invent something and you have it in every paper. My contract is concrete. I am not going anywhere else.'

Williams backed his man, saying: 'I am delighted with Jacques. He is a rookie in F1 and to be second in the world championship after half a season says it all.'

Hill ducked the issue, saying he was only concentrating on winning. As he stood in the paddock, fans stood glued to the mesh fences, gazing in at the elite world of the motor homes and pits and Hill said: 'It really is uplifting at this race. It gives me an extra buzz to be here. There is pressure but I try to use it positively. I know Jacques wants to reverse the situation from Canada, rewrite the script, but it is up to me not to let him do that.'

Now the idea of being a British summer sporting hero appealed.'Nick Faldo is here and he has just won his third Masters, the England football team just failed to beat Germany and I am having a pretty good year so far. I will do everything I can to win Silverstone for a second time.'

By the end of qualifying on Saturday, the football analogy seemed apt for it was quite simply 'Williams 2: The Rest 0'. A 54,000 strong crowd had appeared to watch and if they were there to see British glory, they were delighted.

Schumacher went on pole with his first flying lap and Hill failed to match that. Villeneuve did. Hill then took first place and the Williams had staked out their territory. With fifteen minutes to go, Hill hammered out a 1 minute 26.785 second lap, and despite Villeneuve's best efforts he finished 0.196 behind.

An unexpected bonus for the Williams team was that the Benettons, which test as much at Silverstone and would have been expected to be at home there, were well off the pace, leaving Jean Alesi to describe it as a 'nightmare' to be fifth.

Schumacher was third, almost a second behind, and felt he had got the maximum out of the car to be there. Hill described qualifying as 'a bit of fun' with the real business to come and he congratulated his team on overcoming a tricky day. 'They are really on song, the atmosphere is great.'

Villeneuve had enjoyed a good battle. He had felt he could be on pole. Still, his problems were as nothing compared to the Forti team, who did not run on the Friday because of takeover talks in Italy. Both cars then had limited engine time due to unpaid bills with Cosworth and did not qualify after stopping on the circuit and, on the way home, their transporter was involved in a crash.

Hill blasted so-called fans who had attacked Michael Schumacher's fan-club motor home in a car park, saying: 'We want a good atmosphere here. I want nothing to do with jingoism or misplaced nationalism or hatred of any kind. I reject all those things.

'These people are just hooligans not supporters.'

Schumacher echoed that, adding: 'Our sport is about different fans standing together waving their flags in support of different drivers.'

Pitched Off!

On Sunday, before the British race, came news of even more exotic travel for the F1 circus in 1998 after Korea (South) signed a deal. But the only travelling Hill was worried about was going round 61 laps of Silverstone safely, speedily and in first place. Surely this was to be his day. The dominant man of the season who had triumphed in Australia, Brazil, Argentina, San Marino, Canada and France was coming home, to use the football language of the moment, and he wanted to show 90,000 paying fans how he had done it.

The scene looked perfect. Union Jacks flew high and cheers exploded from the grandstands as Damon Hill waved from the pits, but a closer study revealed the cruel reality. The face was drawn, the smile was strained, the eyes looked tired and he responded to the fans' greetings in a slow, apologetic way – for the fear that had played on his mind during the euphoric build-up to the British Grand Prix had materialised in dramatic fashion.

The plan, according to Hill's supporters, was that their man, who had seized pole position, would be out of sight long before the end of the race. He was, but sadly for him that was because he was in a saloon car, not the Williams. The FW18 was already being probed by mechanics to discover why it had deposited the world championship leader in the gravel at Copse Corner on the 26th lap.

Hill had reminded those in his company during the days before Silverstone that this would be no foregone conclusion. Told that his team-mate Jacques Villeneuve had plans to rip up the script, Hill insisted: 'I have to make sure that does not happen.'

He knew where the real attack would come from – not from outsiders. On a day when Ferrari again astonished race fans and horrified Italy, he was proved correct.

'What can I say?' said Hill after his 400-yard walk back to his garage from his abandoned car. 'That's motor racing. I thought there was something wrong with the car after four or five laps and got on the radio to warn them I had a problem with the front wheel. Then something seized up as I came into Copse. It just pitched me off the road, and that was that.'

Within hours, Williams tracked the cause of despair to a front left wheel-nut which had come loose and was prevented from coming off altogether by a locking device. As Hill braked going into Copse, only the right-hand brakes worked and he spun into the deep gravel. 'It is a real shame. I know I was about 20 seconds behind Jacques, but with a one-stop strategy I felt there was every chance I could have gone on to win. I really, really wanted to win here but it was not to be.'

Villeneuve, so disappointed to lose to Hill at his own home race in Canada one month previously, reversed the start and finish from that race in Montreal to capture the British title. He roared off the grid and as Hill – with a heavier fuel load – made a sorry start, the French-Canadian took the lead with three others also outpacing the Englishman into the first corner. 'The start was very important,' confirmed Villeneuve later, 'because I have the same weapon as Damon, the same car, same engine. I did not care why he had a bad start . . . I was just happy about it.

'Even if he had got in front, we had a good set-up on the car and I think I could have raced him.'

That shows the level of competition Hill faced from his young team-mate, who had no intention of surrendering the fight for the world title. One week earlier, pit-lane gossip had it that the Indycar champion would be replaced at Williams by the end of the year. But Villeneuve scorned the suggestion and the second win of the season which narrowed the championship gap to 15 points indicated his attitude.

Hill had begun the day 25 points to the good, but Villeneuve was quick to point out: 'On a day like today that can disappear very quickly. I know Silverstone well from testing there, but I don't know the next two tracks at Germany and Hungary. But we have eaten into some of Damon's lead.'

Hill remained philosophical as he packed his bags and headed away from the circuit with wife Georgie to meet up with their children.

'Nothing is taken 100 per cent for granted or reliable in motor-racing,' he said as the cars continued to the conclusion of the 61-lap race. 'You cannot predict what will happen. I just have to press on and have my eyes on the next Grand Prix in two weeks at Hockenheim. I am sorry for my supporters. I got a fantastic reception from the crowd and am very grateful for their support.'

Ferrari expected little of that on their own return home. Yet again they had hardly begun the race before they were back in the pits. At least this time, unlike in France a fortnight earlier, Michael Schumacher got to race. They had promised an improvement on failing to last the parade lap at Magny-Cours, but this time the hydraulic system failed and locked the car in sixth gear as the world champion ran fourth. He lasted seven minutes before returning to the pits, while team-mate Eddie

Irvine went positively long distance – six laps – before limping in to join the wake.

'Absurd,' declared Schumacher, whose drive shaft had fallen off in Canada. He had now managed just 44 laps in three races. 'The team is more down than I am. But in racing, things like this can happen even if it seems very strange. We have covered high mileage in testing and have run here for two days without problems.'

Ferrari sporting director Jean Todt, who was given Schumacher's backing two weeks previously when the Italians called for his head, admitted: 'It is a nightmare. To draw conclusions after these terrible six weeks does not seem right to me. I feel sorry for the fans but we were competitive at the start of the season and will be even more so for the rest of the season.'

Their departure left the door open for Benetton, and Jean Alesi looked hot for second place until his brakes started to smoke and out he went. Team-mate Gerhard Berger moved up to finish 19 seconds behind Villeneuve. Mika Hakkinen, who was being hounded by Hill until the Williams broke down, took third in his McLaren Mercedes.

Jordan, who organised the post-race paddock rock'n'roll party, finally had something to sing about with Rubens Barrichello in fourth spot and Martin Brundle sixth. David Coulthard completed the joy for McLaren with fifth place. The last of the home drivers, Johnny Herbert, brought his Sauber Ford in ninth.

Villeneuve departed for his home in Monaco with stewards deliberating on his victory after a technical protest about an aerodynamic fixture on his car. But the word soon came over that the protest had been overruled. Benetton had lodged an official complaint that the front-end wing plates – the small vertical panels holding the struts in place – were too thick.

Hill, a lead guitarist in 1995's paddock concert, had also left. His mind was on other things for, as he admitted: 'There is going to be a tough battle for the rest of the season. You will get retirements now and again. Ferrari have had it a lot worse than we have.

'I must look ahead. The final few races are going to be exciting – but not in the way I would have wanted.'

Race 10: British Grand Prix

Result	Drivers (overall)	Constructors (overall)
1. Jacques Villeneuve (Can)	1. Hill 63	1. Williams 111
2. Gerhard Berger (Aut)	2. Villeneuve 48	2. Benetton 41
3. Mika Hakkinen (Fin)	3. Schumacher 26	3. Ferrari 35
4. Rubens Barrichello (Bra)		
5. David Coulthard (GB)		
6. Martin Brundle (GB)		

12

Seven Up!

German Grand Prix, Hockenheim: 28 July

The disappointment of Hill with his Silverstone setback was nothing to the shock he had of turning up at Hockenheim with questions about his future ringing in his ears and a headline 'Frentzen to take Hill's Williams seat' emblazoned in the leading motorsport magazine. Andrew Benson of *Autosport* had been tipped off by a 'source' in the week before the German race that Frank Williams had already done a deal to sign Germany's Heinz-Harald Frentzen, the same man who had been rumoured to be taking over Villeneuve's seat two weeks earlier.

It did not depend on the popular theory that Hill had to win the championship to be safe. It was a done deal. Not only would Williams not entertain a pay rise for Hill, he simply had decided to bring in a driver he had admired for some time, i.e. Frentzen. The story was picked up all round by national newspapers and Hill was less than enthralled to be faced with such a story as he tried to get back on track. Benson was criticised roundly by many who forgot to apologise later as the story developed and proved to be correct.

At the time, however, it seemed absurd to most people that there was any possibility that a man who was poised to win the world championship would be dropped. They had probably forgotten Nigel Mansell's departure from the team in 1992, the year he won the world title.

'I haven't bothered to read any newspapers,' insisted Hill in Germany. 'The only thing I have to say is that Frank and myself are united in a common goal which is to win the drivers' championship and the constructors' championship for Williams.

141

I am very, very happy at the moment. I am leading the world championship.

'Right now, there's no news for me to give you. The only thing I can say is that winning the championship would give me a lot of options. And that's my goal.

'I'm not going to be drawn into discussing the conjecture as to my future in Grand Prix racing. I have made it clear many times before that I would love to stay at Williams. I have not driven seriously for any other Formula One team and I feel very much part of the team. A lot of the success we've had this year has been brought about through my hard work and application, and working with the team and being a good team member. I would hate for that to change.'

Frank Williams did not exactly deny it but he did say: 'The Rothmans Williams Renault team has only one job in hand at this stage of the season, that is to secure the constructors' championship and to give our drivers the best possible opportunity of securing the drivers' championship.

'Jacques Villeneuve having commenced a two-year contract with the team at the beginning of the 1996 season is the only confirmed driver for 1997. Negotiations regarding the team's other driver for 1997 will commence in good time.'

It should have been a relief for Hill to get into the car but Germany had never been a happy hunting ground for him. He had won in a dozen countries but never Germany, and the previous year had lasted just two laps until he delighted the howling mob by spinning off. The crowd have always taken a keen delight in making life noisy and uncomfortable for Hill at Hockenheim and this was no exception.

'I've never been to Hockenheim,' confessed Villeneuve. 'It's a pretty quick track but it is not too complex to drive. I am looking forward eagerly to the race – it is a downforce circuit and we have plenty of that. I had tested a lot at Silverstone and there my start was crucial but the next two rounds are on new circuits to me. I have eaten into Damon's lead and will keep pushing.'

Major Boost

Hill led his team-mate by just 15 points and beat him in the practice session, finishing eighth to Villeneuve's eleventh. Bursting with confidence after his win at Silverstone, the young French-Canadian believed the result of the race would settle the destination of the world title.

'It is going to be the crucial race of the season,' he said. 'I believe I can beat Damon in a straight fight. Why shouldn't I? Silverstone was a straight fight to the first corner and then Damon got stuck in traffic. The first corner is very important in determining the result.'

Villeneuve's self-confidence was at a peak, and after seeing Hill off on his home turf he knew a repeat performance would unsettle the leader and set up a nail-biting finale to the season.

'I feel more and more assured and experienced,' said Villeneuve. 'Picking up 10 points in Britain helped a lot and I find it is getting easier with every race. No Grand Prix is easy, but I don't have to concentrate on learning so many new things. I'm working with the team and getting used to the car.'

Germany was especially important to him since he knew the subsequent Grands Prix in Hungary and Belgium might not be to his liking. But Hockenheim's long straights suited his blistering speed and keeping so close to Hill in practice was a major boost.

The Briton had even more to prove after the disappointment of Silverstone. Hill was not happy with eighth in practice – one behind Michael Schumacher.

'The car's not perfect but with new tyres I can be optimistic for qualifying,' he said. 'We have a lot of work to do but I am certain we can get the car good in time.'

Schumacher, roared on by home support that bordered on the religious, admitted his troubled times at Ferrari might not be over.

'It was not fun for me out there at all,' he said. 'I haven't sorted the car out yet. I was all over the place. Something's not right but I don't know what it is. It could be the rear end or the front end or both. I just don't know.'

His fans were desperate for a repeat of 1995's victory, when he became the first German to win on home ground. Both days in 1996 were 125,000 sell-outs for several months in advance. But he showed little sign of his disappointment at the likely loss of his world crown and failure to finish his last three races.

'Crisis? There is no crisis,' he said. 'I still want to win a couple of races before the end of the season and the team, like me, are confident we can do that.'

That confidence increased after team-mate Eddie Irvine set the third fastest practice time in the other Ferrari. Schumacher said: 'I will have a glance at Eddie's set-up which should help me in qualifying.'

The Benetton drivers, Gerhard Berger and Jean Alesi, finished first and fourth respectively, with Scotsman David Coulthard second in the McLaren.

The next day Hill punched the air in utter delight and relief after a qualifying session he marked out as one of the most exciting he could remember. The gesture also seemed to be testimony to more than his pole position. It was the celebration of reclamation of the high ground after failing to finish in Britain and a barrage of questions over his future. All weekend he had been hounded by Frentzen's name. Hill chose to respond on the circuit. His decisive lap in qualifying usurped Michael Schumacher seconds from the end and the German's disappointment was heightened when Austria's Gerhard Berger relegated him to third place.

A buoyant Hill said: 'It has been just a brilliant day. I don't waste my time worrying about what other people say about my future. My only concern is about this race and the run-in to the championship. I've been confident all weekend. It was a last-minute effort but I knew we had the right equipment to do it. The whole team have done a fantastic job.'

Hill, who had had to have guards to protect him on at least one previous visit, was now a big fan of the atmosphere at Hockenheim, where the final loops of the circuit are guarded by concrete stands which are packed.

'I wish we could have more tracks with a stadium area like this,' he said. 'You can feel the tension as you drive out there and it adds so much to the place.'

Even a protest by Minardi that Hill had ignored a red light at the weighbridge, an offence which might have left him at the back of the grid, could not detract from his pleasure. After hearing evidence from Hill and the team manager Dickie Standford, the stewards accepted that the stop light had been turned on too late for him to see it as he passed.

Frentzen's name was also linked with McLaren as part of a deal to extend that team's partnership with Mercedes and that posed the question of whether David Coulthard would move to the new Stewart Grand Prix team. Ulsterman Eddie Irvine was under pressure to keep his place at Ferrari because the team was being urged by the Italian media to enrol a local hero – but that rumour was squashed on Sunday when he was confirmed for the following year.

Hill's concerns eased throughout the session. To complete the day, his team-mate and closest title rival Jacques Villeneuve qualified in a modest sixth. Given a clean start and no mechanical problems, Hill seemed likely to extend his 15-point advantage.

Berger Blow

Yet again, however, he blew the start. Too much wheelspin cost all the good work of the day before and it looked ominous as both Benettons leapt past, Berger taking the lead and Hill settling in behind Alesi.

He had another problem for it became clear that the B196s were on a one-stop strategy and Hill was on two. Hill stopped on lap 20, 16 seconds clear of Schumacher and rejoined fifth. When the Benettons stopped for a wash and wipe, Hill was ahead and began whipping round at up to 2 seconds a lap faster.

Another stop for Hill on lap 34 and he was out between the

two Benettons, close to Berger but the experienced front man was determined to wipe away the agonies of a bitterly poor season by winning what is currently his home Grand Prix, there being no Austrian event until 1997. There seemed no way past for Hill, the Renault-powered cars were equal for power and Berger blocked within the bounds of acceptability. Still, second would provide 6 points for Hill, not ideal but not bad.

Then, suddenly, a puff of smoke and as if by magic Damon Hill sprung into view and into the lead.

When Gerhard Berger's engine finally buckled under pressure with two-and-a-half laps of the German Grand Prix remaining, Hill emerged with a clear run to his seventh win of the season. Hill was forced to play a tactical game of patience after surrendering pole position advantage at the first corner, sitting behind the breakaway Benettons of Berger and Jean Alesi, while the rest of the pack dropped further behind. But Hill's persistence was rewarded with a 21-point lead in the drivers' championship and a landmark twentieth Grand Prix win. Sweeter, perhaps, was the taste of his first victory on German soil – soil which happened to be Michael Schumacher's back garden – when thousands were willing the reigning champion's resurrection from Ferrari hell.

'It was a bloody good win,' Hill said. 'It was a fantastic race and I could not feel any better. It was going to be difficult after my bad start and by the end it needed an error from Gerhard. I don't think I could have passed him. It is a damn shame for him, but I have a lot to celebrate.'

As if coping with over 190 miles of driving was not enough, Hill even had to dodge accusations of being fortunate to take the 10 points.

'No way was I lucky,' he said, stunned by the suggestion. 'I have had my fair share of bad luck before. This was a very timely result and it was crucial for me to get the points.'

The enormous crowd might have been denied the thrill of seeing Hill overtaking for victory, but the suddenness of Berger's departure was no less spectacular. For a moment, Hill was obscured as smoke belched out of the Benetton, but the fog neither broke his admirable concentration nor swayed him from his relentless charge to the world title.

'Coming out of the chicane, we both accelerated,' explained Hill. 'I heard one of the engines make a bad noise and I thought at first it might have been mine. But I moved to the right just in time to avoid being drowned in smoke.'

He finished covered instead in champagne and glory.

Berger said: 'I am very sad because I wanted the victory so much. I looked in good shape and could not believe what happened. Everything looked perfect and I was confident that I could have held off Damon, as I had done the previous 10 laps.

'I had no warning that anything was wrong until suddenly the engine blew. What more can I say? *C'est la vie.'*

A good day for the Williams team was made better by Jacques Villeneuve's gutsy drive into third place – behind Alesi – which kept the pressure on his team-mate for the final five races and took Williams to within 2 points of the constructors' title.

Yet Germany had hoped for a different script, aching for the home-grown hero Schumacher to surge to the fore on the tide of fervour sweeping down from the grandstands. In the end, it rained on his parade. Schu-mania peaked as he drove around the Hockenheimring before the race, waving regally from a classic open-topped Ferrari. The Popemobile itself could not have received a more reverent reception. But perhaps angered by the religious imagery, the heavens opened with a vengeance. It might have signalled a boost for Schumacher as his only victory thus far had been at Barcelona under similar skies. But when the sun came out, it chose to shine on Hill.

Even a pre-race kiss from another returning local hero, Boris Becker, could not push the Ferrari to victory, a case of Boom-Boom failing to inspire Vroom Vroom. Schumacher was left to battle it out with McLaren's David Coulthard for much of the race, holding off the Scot to finish fourth, 41 seconds behind Hill.

The German said: 'I am disappointed to have finished so far back, but at the same time it was important to see the chequered flag again. The car was better here than at the last few races, apart from the brakes which gave me problems.

'The support from the public helped me a lot. They even gave me a warm reception for fourth place.'

For Hill, the championship was now there for the losing, although he knew the title he craved might have to wait a few more races.

'You only have to look at Silverstone to realise how one non-finish allows the other guys to close up on you very quickly,' he said.

It had been a tough week at the office. Reports that he might be dropped by Williams for 1997 failed to destabilise him. Indeed, it emerged that a herculean team effort through the night back at the Williams factory in Oxfordshire had induced some last-minute aerodynamic improvements in the car. New parts were flown to Germany on the morning of the race, and a grateful Hill said: 'I can't tell you what the changes were but they made a big difference.'

Frank Williams acclaimed Hill for his brilliant charge in the closing stages. 'That was vintage stuff from Damon,' he said. 'He really did the team proud. He made the most of both his sets of new tyres and did a fantastic job to get hold of it after a poor start.'

Villeneuve, who had no previous experience of Hockenheim, was disappointed not to have narrowed the gap on Hill in the title race.

'I was looking to win, but it didn't happen,' he said. 'With five races to go, I am still in with a chance and will keep fighting to the end.'

Hill, meanwhile, had just one thought in mind. 'My future?' he queried wearily for the fourth time in as many days. 'I will go back to the trailer, get changed, have a drink and shake the hand of everyone on the team.'

Becker and opera star Placido Domingo presented the trophies on the podium but Hill was not counting the title as his until the fat lady sang and there was no sign of her, just yet.

Race 11: German Grand Prix

Result	Drivers (overall)	Constructors (overall)
1. Damon Hill (GB)	1. Hill 73	1. Williams 125
2. Jean Alesi (Fra)	2. Villeneuve 52	2. Benetton 47
3. Jacques Villeneuve (Can)	3. Alesi 31	3. Ferrari 38
4. Michael Schumacher (Ger)		
5. David Coulthard (GB)		
6. Rubens Barrichello (Bra)		

13

Disgust And Defeat

Hungarian Grand Prix, Budapest: 11 August

The champagne was on ice as the Williams team began their unpacking in the usual soaring temperatures of central Europe in August, for this was the weekend when their ambition would be rewarded with the transition from good to great. The team required just 2 points to clinch the championship Frank Williams really cared about. Most of the talk in Formula One revolves around drivers and their titles but Williams made no bones about it: 'The one I want is the constructors' championship.'

It was not simply that Williams would again be the best of the constructors for their eighth title. Success would put the Oxfordshire team alongside Ferrari who held the record. What an achievement that would be twenty-seven years after the team started with just £30,000 scraped together and now running with a budget closer to £30 million a year. The last time Ferrari had won the constructors' title had been in 1983, and since then Williams had secured it five times. Long gone were the days when Frank operated from above a garage in Slough, when he had his telephone cut off and used a public phone box to run the team, had to borrow money to get out of the airport car park after a race and saw creditors far more often than sponsors.

'I started off with Piers Courage in a Formula Three race as a one-off,' Williams recalled as he sat at the track, clad as usual in his blue, v-neck sweater, white shirt and grey flannels, operating from a wheelchair.

'I don't really remember what it was like in the past but

151

there is absolutely no way I look back on them as the good old days. I never gave up hope of making it but the plan then was just to get to the next race. There is more to enjoy now: more cars, more people, more success.'

With his co-director Patrick Head, the brilliant designer who joined in 1977, he had created a team which retained much of its English attitudes but dominated one of the world's fiercest technological battlegrounds, not just once as so often happens, but for a long time. There had been five Williams world champions: Alan Jones, Keke Rosberg, Nelson Piquet, Nigel Mansell and Alain Prost but Williams had never hidden his ambition from the men he hired to drive the supercar.

'I will be thrilled to bits to win the constructors' championship,' he said. 'That is always what has been most important to me. It is a team business and I am not here for the benefit of the drivers. I am here to enjoy myself and keep up my living. The drivers come and go but the team is here forever.'

Words that would echo in a few heads within weeks for Hill was just beginning his salary negotiations for 1997. 'I have spoken to Frank,' he said after arriving in Hungary. 'We have on-going discussions and I think things are going well on that front. It is not the main topic on my mind, though.'

Negotiation is a dangerous business and dealing with a man who is so matter-of-fact about life, who has bravely overcome a frightful accident, whose direct answers startle newcomers, would not be easy, especially as Frank had the best car. Williams is quiet, modest and is an expert at the British art of understatement. He has his aims in perspective and there it takes a good deal of genuine human achievement to really impress the great man whose talent to infuriate is almost as great as his ability to organise a team of 250, now working from a state-of-the-art factory in Grove, teaching other British businesses how to do it.

The only mystery was why Williams had never been knighted but it is hardly something he worries about. As long as the Williams cars are leading, he is happy and so Hill duly obliged, ripping through a late practice lap on Friday to put Schumacher into second place.

Hill was less perturbed about the world champion, languishing 44 points behind him, than about Villeneuve who had never driven on the dusty, slippy circuit before but had already mastered it enough to be just 0.2 seconds behind.

A Race to the End

The Hungaroring is a nicely laid out circuit, good for spectators, sun tans and goulash but less attractive for overtaking on a narrow, twisting track. The traffic jams on the motorway outside are often emulated on the circuit as car follows car for lap after lap. Yet it has been memorable for the British drivers, particularly Nigel Mansell who clinched his 1992 world title over the 72 laps, and to Damon Hill, who won his first Grand Prix near Budapest in 1993.

'It has a feel-good factor about it,' Hill said as he looked across the hills which give the circuit its rolling characteristic. 'I feel very familiar with it. I don't really know what it is, but it is there.'

It wasn't quite there on Saturday, however, when qualifying rolled along and Hill admitted that he never felt he had done a 'real peach of a lap' and was happy enough to settle for second, a mere 0.053 seconds behind Schumacher but only 0.077 seconds ahead of his team-mate. Villeneuve had settled in extremely well, described the place as fun and was giving it a big blast.

Down on the Danube in Budapest on Saturday night, Hill could contemplate a tough race ahead but he would not have dreamed that his start could be so bad on a sunny Sunday. It spoiled his chances as a winner there and then, leaving Hill struggling all day to overcome the handicap.

He tried, he really worked and after 77 laps the gap was agonisingly small, a mere fingertip in Formula One language, a stretch across a divide that separated Damon Hill not just from the car in front but to the handle of the trophy that filled his waking hours, his dreaming nights.

Just 120 feet after 185 miles and not much less than two hours in the sweltering heat that shimmered in the hills north of Budapest, a stretch of ground which his supercar could cover in less than a second, in the time it takes to blink. Yet as desperate as Hill was to close that gap, his rival Jacques Villeneuve displayed enough determination and skill to ensure that the Briton was frustrated, his ambition to win the Hungarian Grand Prix and then the next race in Belgium to clinch the world championship left in limbo.

'That's the best second place I have ever had in my life,' said Hill with a shake of his head as Villeneuve sipped champagne in the motor home. Around the Rothmans Williams Renault area, there was no shortage of good cheer, for their fifth 1-2 finish of the year had clinched the world constructors' championship by some margin. Now they were up there with Ferrari's record. It was no small achievement and neither Hill nor his French-Canadian team-mate played down that success, but their minds were clearly moving on to more personal battles for they were the only two men who could now lay claim to the drivers' title.

Hill had never been under any illusion about the challenge, but now he knew that Villeneuve was back to his best, holding off first Michael Schumacher and then the 35-year-old Englishman on a tricky, twisting, swooping circuit. Villeneuve was happy to make his ambitions and feelings as clear as Hungarian crystal, and Hill's 21-point lead, now reduced to 17, might be as fragile.

Even team director Patrick Head admitted: 'I would rather be the one leading by 17 points but if at the next race Jacques wins and Damon has a technical problem and does not finish, then it is only 7 points and that could disappear very quickly in the final three races. It is very interesting. It could well be a race to the end.'

Hill was considering the same problem but his own driving in Hungary should not be underestimated after a start which he himself described as 'disgusting' although pointing out that it was a clutch problem more than a personal failing. This problem has wounded Hill too often, not fatally but he has bled points and places. He had been concentrating on his start, he told me, after losing out on pole at the German Grand Prix but 'again I had a poor start and paid the price. I lost the race in the first 10 laps, it was over then. Jacques and Michael were long gone.'

Starting second behind Schumacher on the dirtier side of the track, Hill found his wheels spinning, tried to compensate on the clutch and watched in bitter agony as first Villeneuve accelerated past and then Benetton's Jean Alesi.

The Frenchman has the same engine and great talent but is handicapped by a less efficient car and Hill found himself swallowing Alesi's dust for 22 slow laps until the Benetton pitted and by then Schumacher and Villeneuve were out of sight 21 seconds clear.

'I was pretty happy at Damon's start,' said Villeneuve candidly. 'I knew that Jean would almost certainly make a good start and that would make sure that Damon went slowly at least until his first pit stop. That would give us good space and be good for the championship.'

Hill would beg to differ and once he was released from Alesi's prison, he spent the rest of the day proving that he was the fastest driver on the circuit. Even then, he did so despite a change of strategy that surprised him when the team decided in mid-race to switch Hill from two stops to three which further frustrated the driver who admitted later: 'It was a bit confusing about what was going on.

'I thought I knew what was happening until they asked me to stop for a second time and then I found I was doing another.

'I would have preferred two stops. I think that would have been better, saving an extra 30 seconds. Anyway, I pushed as hard as I could to make up as much ground as I could.'

There is no argument with that for, having set the fastest time on lap 23, Hill followed up with four fastest laps on 32, 34, 35 and 36 as he hared after the men who were thwarting his title ambitions.

Two laps later he was the sole object of Union Jack attention as Johnny Herbert pulled up to join Martin Brundle, whose Jordan bucked and crashed to a halt, David Coulthard whose engine seized on the 23rd lap and Eddie Irvine, a victim again of Ferrari's mechanical failings.

Hill powered on, reeling in Schumacher at up to 3 seconds a lap, then did it all over again after a 42nd-lap pit-stop, melting an 11.6 second deficit to virtually zero with fierce driving until the German pitted. That put Hill behind Villeneuve, albeit a long way. Villeneuve had a worrying stop when a faulty wheel nut cost him valuable seconds in the pits at a tyre change and when Hill emerged after his halt with 13 laps to go, the battle was on.

Slowly but surely Villeneuve's lead whittled away, from 6.6 seconds to a fraction over a single second on the 71st lap when the 110,000 crowd, mainly comprising Germans and Italians it seemed from the klaxons and flags, were silenced yet again when a throttle control problem saw the Prancing Horse of Ferrari led to the stable early yet again.

Hill reduced the gap to 0.608 of a second on the penultimate lap but Villeneuve was in control with, as he admitted, the same weapon and crossed the line 40 yards, 0.771 seconds ahead.

'It was tough at the end when Damon was pushing,' said Villeneuve. 'I had to get myself in to pushing mode, too.

'At the start I was pushing Michael but there was not a gap big enough to get by. It was close but it was fun because I was pushing and he was sliding quite a bit and making mistakes.

'I am delighted to have won and this will certainly make the championship exciting.'

The margins were tiny, so fine that Hill left for a promotional tour of Bulgaria knowing that he couldn't afford to measure his cabinet just yet for the trophy for which he had twice been runner-up to Schumacher.

The German's reign finished in Hungary when he lost his last utterly forlorn hope of a miracle but just who would follow Schumacher's name onto the trophy remained a mystery which promised to be a thriller.

Under Pressure

Patrick Head reiterated that there would be no team orders for the final four races and added: 'In the earlier part of the season I used to say "there are no team orders but please don't have each other off" but I got bored with saying that.

'They know it goes without saying. I went over and had a word with Frank before the end of the race when it was very close between them and said "If you want to go out into the pit lane and hang out a notice saying how it should be" but he said "No, no, no" and we let them get on with it.

'Anyway, it would be a waste of time. We would have two blind drivers.

'Jacques is a serious competitor to Damon now. Earlier this year there was a period when he was not quite as close but he seems to have raised his game. His poorer performance may have been a technical thing. When Damon's race engineer, David Brown, left for McLaren, Tim Preston started work on Damon's car. Tim is very good technically but Damon was worried that he might lose out because of Tim's inexperience.

'Adrian Newey has been to a lot of races this year and we asked him to pay particular attention to Damon's car and I think Damon benefited from that. Jacques hasn't always had Adrian available to him. Maybe that's a factor, maybe not.'

After the race, Hill went to Bulgaria, Villeneuve to Monaco but there was no hint of banishment for the runner-up, simply a promotional trip for Rothmans. They both had the same thought in mind: 'I can win the title.'

Hill, however, could see Villeneuve looming large in his mirrors now for, as he pointed out: 'Jacques may not know the next circuit in Spa, although that was not a problem in Hungary, but he does know the last three at Monza, Portugal and Japan.

'I don't think the extra pressure will affect our relationship. We have a dig at each other but in the best spirit. Nevertheless, he wants to win the title and so do I, so we will watch each other. I think I deserve the title. I am going to have to hang on till the grim death.'

Villeneuve was just as determined and even jauntier. 'I surprised myself in Hungary because I do not normally learn slow circuits so quickly. This win was my best so far because I beat Damon fair and square.

'The championship is wide open. The plan is to take it down to the wire. It would be nice if Damon suffered some mishaps but it is impossible to predict that.'

Hill, disappointed, was determined to look ahead. He felt comfortable with his position and now talks had started with Frank Williams. A temporary setback but the future looked rosy... or did it?

Race 12: Hungarian Grand Prix

Result	Drivers (overall)	Constructors (overall)
1. Jacques Villeneuve (Can)	1. Hill 79	1. Williams 141
2. Damon Hill (GB)	2. Villeneuve 62	2. Benetton 51
3. Jean Alesi (Fra)	3. Alesi 35	3. Ferrari 38
4. Mika Hakkinen (Fin)		
5. Olivier Panis (Fra)		
6. Rubens Barrichello (Bra)		

14

Radio Daze

The delights of Belgium lured Damon to Spa in good form as would be expected of someone who had won twice in 1993 and 1994 and come second last year, a formidable record on a spectacular circuit, the last of the giants. Spa-Francorchamps in late August has a touch of early autumn about it, for the weather is always unpredictable, the setting beautiful in the forests of the Ardennes and the racing fast and thrilling.

A run round in a hired Fiat Punto, or on the back of a scooter as last year, was exciting and inspiring enough for me. Travelling at up to 190 mph in a racing car for 44 laps of the 4.3 mile circuit, the longest on the calendar, was a true test of the imagination.

Plunging downhill past the stands to the Eau Rouge corner, along the fast straight, up and down genuine hills, round hairpins like La Source, your stomach moving, your head jerking around, it is impossible to imagine what sort of battering a driver takes during the lap of around 1 minute 28 seconds if you are in one of the quicker cars.

Hill had spent time at the Williams test session in Jerez in southern Spain working on his standing starts. He had tried ten but with limited success although he believed he had found some things which could be useful.

'It is a question of balance between the technical side and adapting my technique with the clutch,' he said. 'I am more confident now about getting the car off the line. There is no question that if I do get away, then I will be difficult to beat.'

He dismissed the idea of switching to a hand clutch like

159

Villeneuve's, comparing it to trying to write with your left hand if you are right-handed.

'I am a right foot braker and I cannot adapt,' he said. 'I just don't have the feel in my left foot. I raced bikes and did not do karting before I came into cars and I prefer a foot clutch.'

Patrick Head had considered the problem of Hill's poor starting and admitted that he had been brilliant in 1993 but had fallen away since then. 'Perhaps we have fallen behind McLaren and Benetton in the technology while we worked on other areas, it is difficult to tell,' he said. 'Maybe it is just a question of confidence.'

Hill's aim was to finish off the championship as rapidly as possible. He had many fears but never did Damon Hill expect to be handicapped by the man who designed the supercar which had reduced the championship to a two-man race for the Williams team.

On the Limit

Hill was totally focused but Schumacher became totally unfocused for a few seconds on Friday when he provided the big crash of the weekend in the morning session, losing control at the Fagnes downhill left hander in the closing moments. The car jerked, spun and hurtled backwards into a tyre wall at 100 mph. The back of the Ferrari was destroyed and although Schumacher climbed out, he limped away and did not appear for the afternoon session, opting to sleep off the effects and nursing a heavily bruised thigh which had broken the steering wheel on impact.

He still managed to end up second fastest though, his car being fitted with the latest seven-speed gearbox. Hill was seventh at the end and talked of the circuit as 'awe-inspiring' but the big story which seeped from Spa-Francorchamps was of McLaren considering offering Hill a £10 million deal for 1997.

Within days of the Belgian race, the worst kept secret in F1 was confirmed when Marlboro announced the end of their long-standing sponsorship of the team, taking their £20 million a year elsewhere. McLaren promptly launched a five-year sponsorship with a German tobacco company and from 1997 would be known as West McLaren Mercedes. They needed to make an impact and if Hill won the title, the theory was, he could be lured with the number one on the car, also keeping out Ralf Schumacher, Michael's younger brother, who had recently tested for the team, and providing a strong British line-up. Not ideal for Mercedes but good for Ron Dennis, the McLaren boss, who would still be a master of his own fate.

Dennis declined to deny or confirm interest in Hill, saying merely that David Coulthard would definitely stay with the team but negotiations were on with the current driver, Mika Hakkinen, and they would seek the 'best available driver' for the following season.

Mercedes happened to be one of three rebel teams who had decided not to sign the Concorde Agreement which was to govern all major policy in F1 for five years. Frank Williams had withdrawn his support at the last minute and Ken Tyrrell also declined to stay with the pack. It was all the usual Grand Prix politicking but it meant nothing to most and particularly Villeneuve who, rather worryingly for Hill, was enjoying himself. 'It is a great track, tough to learn but the car is pretty good and it is a great track with a lot of high speed turns that are very demanding – so it is fun.

'Eau Rouge is a strange corner because you are going downhill and you can just see a wall in front of you that goes up. Once you get into it, you have to change direction just when the track starts going up. You just bottom out, it gets pretty heavy and you can't see the exit. But you can always go faster, that's the weird thing.

'You think you are on the limit, then you try it faster and the car is even more stable. It is great.'

Villeneuve's comments were interesting about the change in the set-up of his car and how things had developed over the year. 'We are basically using the same settings as Damon. I have always worked the same way but now with the end of the season in sight, the chemistry is better with the engineers and the rest of the team. The trust is higher, too.'

Had the battle changed his relationship with Damon?

'No, we are competitors. We don't hate each other's guts, there is no reason for that. He is a nice guy and we get along very well. But that is where it stops.'

He ended the practice day third to Hill's seventh but the most original quote for not doing well, give or take the odd translation difficulty, came from Giovanni Lavaggi of Minardi who was last and said: 'I was abandoned by my engine at the last chicane.' Some cars just know when to call a halt.

Villeneuve's good mood and great form continued through the Saturday morning warm-up and into the qualifying session when everyone took a look at the sky with the squadrons of grey clouds building over the hills and headed for their cars.

If there was a downpour, those who set the fast times on dry track would be uncatchable and no one wanted to be caught out. Hill was among the first and Villeneuve failed to beat his team-mate's time and then failed again after the Englishman's second run.

Now Hill made a change to the set-up to try out something new for his third run and that was not as good. Villeneuve seized the opportunity, putting in a fierce lap which pushed him top by four-tenths of a second. Before Hill could respond, the rain exploded and the times were determined.

Schumacher had been canny, too, defying the pain from his Friday crash to eke out third, over seven-tenths behind Hill but his humour had not deserted him and when he arrived in first for the pole position press conference he remarked: 'At least I can be quicker than them once this weekend.'

As if to rub in the defeat of the seasoned campaigners, Villeneuve admitted, albeit a touch reluctantly, his novel way of learning about Spa, a legend in its lap time: 'This might sound a bit childish and stupid but I checked out a new video game.

'The tracks are actually quite close so it gives you a good

idea of where you should be going, but that is about it. I was about 18th – I wasn't very good.'

Hill looked bemused and confessed: 'There is always a certain amount of pain in being beaten. It was an exciting qualifying session but I don't deny I was frustrated when the rain came and I did not get out on my last set of tyres. I usually get a good run on my last set.

'Jacques did a great job to take pole, having never seen the circuit before. That shows how determined he is to win and also how hard I will have to work to try to beat him.'

Costly Mix-up

Work hard he did, but never has Hill been as grateful to his rival, Schumacher, as on this day for it was he who saved him from real championship damage with a superb drive which delighted the thousands of fans who had trekked from Germany and Italy.

Villeneuve drove like the wind, hardly putting a wheel out of place, but Schumacher, still stiff and sore from his crash, took his lead from Olympic double gold medallist Michael Johnson whom he met before the race. Johnson, winner of the 200 and 400 metres in Atlanta, exchanged a pair of purple running shoes for a Schumacher helmet and stood back to watch his motor-racing hero blaze his way to the 21st win of his career.

Hill had many fears about this race, enough to match his hopes, and he worried about his team-mate but he never expected to be handicapped by another area of the Williams outfit. Yet, as a rueful Hill left Belgium, Adrian Newey, who was in charge of the driver's pit team, admitted: 'It was my mistake.'

Hill was left shrugging his shoulders and wondering what went wrong after finishing fifth in the Belgian Grand Prix while Michael Schumacher celebrated his second win of the season and Jacques Villeneuve, the only man who could beat the Englishman for the world title, savoured a second place.

As he headed for a flight home to Dublin, his lead cut from 17 points to 13, Hill was told the circumstances of a one-minute mix-up which wrecked his chances of winning the race and taking a giant step to winning the drivers' championship. The extraordinary mistake came after his team-mate, Villeneuve, had been told to come in first for fresh tyres and more fuel but his radio was not working well and the French-Canadian did not understand the message and carried on for an extra lap.

Hill, who was running fourth, was then ordered in for his stop on lap 13 but as he neared the pit lane entrance, he was suddenly told to carry on. That forced him to weave through an overshoot trap for the chicane and he lost time and places. Villeneuve then heard the message and came in next time round with Hill coming in at the end of the lap 15. By the time he rejoined, he had slipped to twelfth and was then passed briefly by Pedro Diniz and had to begin fighting his way up the field.

It happened as the safety car toured round the Spa circuit after Dutchman Jos Verstappen crashed heavily when his throttle stuck open. He wrote off his Arrows car which caught fire. He was led away groggily from the wreckage and airlifted to hospital for a check-up and the rest of the field had to re-group and circulate behind the official car while the car was moved and the tyre wall rebuilt.

As soon as the yellow warning flag had come out, Schumacher had cleverly dived for the pits and was back out ahead of the Williams men in the queue of cars. Hill, who had made another poor start, dropped from second on the grid behind Villeneuve to third as Schumacher rocketed past and was fourth by the end of the first lap when Scotland's David Coulthard powered through.

The problems had begun even before the race for he had changed cars after a spin in the morning warm-up caused potential damage to the Renault engine. The spare car was not as good, suffered badly from understeer, and Hill did not find it handled as well or was as quick. Yet he could have finished on the podium until the enemy he feared surfaced as his own team.

'Our normal procedure is to call in the man who is leading in the race first and that is what we did when we radioed Jacques,' said Newey.

'Unfortunately his radio did not work very well and he did not hear and went past. He was therefore a lap late in coming in. I called for Damon to come in and then decided that there was not enough time to change over from Jacques' tyres and fuel rig and so I changed my mind and told him to stay out.

'If I could have my time again, I would have stuck to calling him in and we would have swapped the tyres in the pit lane and we would probably have lost less time than we did. He went out twelfth and maybe he would have gone out eighth which might have made a difference to the final placings.

'I made a mistake but there is very little time to think out there. I have spoken to Damon and explained the situation.'

Hill did battle his way up to fifth and although he put a brave face on the situation at the end, he was obviously less than happy at the problems he had suffered.

'If I had pitted as soon as the safety car came out, it would have been much better,' said Hill. 'I was not able to go into the pits when I should have. My intention was to come in and that was the first communication from the team. Then I was told to stay out.

'You would have to ask them what happened. My race changed when the safety car came out. You will have to speak to the team to find out what went on. I was called in, then told to abort and then had to go back out.

'I am just relieved to have got two crucial points. At one stage it looked as if I would not get any. It is the first time in a race here that I was praying for rain. That would have helped.'

He blamed dampness from the morning rain on his side of the grid, as did several others, for another slow start which again cost him a place when Schumacher roared past off the grid pushing Hill, second behind Villeneuve, down to third.

'I had water on my side of the track and made a reasonably good start, considering. David Coulthard got a tow behind

me and coming out of Eau Rouge, he just came straight past –
I was very surprised.

'He was on a one-stop strategy and his performance there
was very impressive. I settled down and kept chasing although
the car was not as good as my original race car.

'It was an interesting race, that's all you can say.

'I still have a lead and Jacques has it all to do. There are
only three races left and somehow that is less daunting than
four.'

Villeneuve also rued the missed message for his stop as he
also blamed that for costing him a win and admitted: 'I picked
up on Damon but 4 points a race is not enough. It was a good
opportunity to get points back but we lost the race through
miscommunication at the pit-stops.

'They were ready but I could not understand what I was
told.'

Schumacher's weekend had started badly with a heavy crash
but he believed that to be a good omen after also having
problems a year ago, starting from sixteenth to win in 1995. In
jocular mood, he had asked a crowd of journalists to help him
out on Saturday night by going out to have plenty of beers
and then coming back to the circuit to soak it by relieving
themselves on the track.

Yet he won in warm sunshine, for once finding a perfect
performance from the Ferrari as it wound its way along the
sweeping bends and soaring hills on the greatest of the tracks
left in Formula One. It was his twenty-first win, taking him
one ahead of Hill again, and he achieved it despite almost
pulling up after damaging the steering on the kerbs as he chased
Villeneuve.

'I was close to stopping because it was a bit frightening,
especially through the Eau Rouge section which is very fast
and tough on the steering,' said Schumacher.

'They told me from the pits that it was not dangerous and I
pushed on. It may have seemed clever to stop when the safety
car came out but it was the fuel tank which made the decision.
It would have been empty if I had gone on.'

And he added pointedly: 'Even if we were not quicker than the Williams, we were able to keep at their pace and we won by doing everything right – the set-up, the strategy and the pit-stops.'

Hill could still win the title at the Italian Grand Prix in Monza if he was first and Villeneuve failed to finish in the top three. He was the only British driver among the ten finishers in Belgium for Coulthard spun off on the 37th lap when he was fifth, ahead of Hill. Eddie Irvine's Ferrari had already succumbed to gearbox trouble, Martin Brundle's Jordan Peugeot had developed engine trouble and poor Johnny Herbert had managed just 200 yards when he and Sauber team-mate Heinz Harald Frentzen collided at the first corner.

Hill's collision was with his team and there would be much debate about future pit-stops in the last three races.

He would simply go home, have some time with the family, have a couple of days testing at the Paul Ricard circuit and head for Monza with a clear, untroubled vision of the future. That was the idea but within three days, his world would explode.

Race 13: Belgian Grand Prix

Result	Drivers (overall)	Constructors (overall)
1. Michael Schumacher (Ger)	1. Hill 81	1. Williams 149
2. Jacques Villeneuve (Can)	2. Villeneuve 68	2. Benetton 55
3. Mika Hakkinen (Fin)	3. Schumacher 39	3. Ferrari 48
4. Jean Alesi (Fra)		
5. Damon Hill (GB)		
6. Gerhard Berger (Aut)		

15

Good Morning . . . Goodbye

Italian Grand Prix, Monza: 8 September

Michael Breen, manager, friend and lawyer for Damon Hill, was in his office in Gray's Inn Road in London where he works as a partner in the legal firm of Edward Lewis. At ten minutes past twelve on Wednesday, 28 August, his secretary put through a telephone call from Frank Williams which changed Hill's life.

'Good morning,'said Williams from his office in the factory at Grove in Oxfordshire.

'Good afternoon,' said Breen in jocular reply. Within seconds he realised Frank was not in a laughing mood.

'What is happening?' asked Breen. To which Williams replied that he had decided to cease negotiations, concerning Hill's contract for 1997.

'Right,' said Breen with commendable calm, so much so that Williams said: 'I have to stress that this is not a negotiating position.'

Breen asked if there was a reason for this state of affairs, to which Williams replied that it was his 'prerogative' and that was that. The next telephone call was a lengthy one from Breen to Hill who reacted exactly the same as his lawyer when he was given the news: 'Right.'

Hill had been in talks and was looking for a considerable rise to boost his status financially. Believed to be on £4.5 million a year, he wanted at least £2 million more. Suggestions flew around that originally he and Breen had talked of asking for £10 million but that would have been a starting figure if used at all.

Later that day, Hill spoke with Williams and again asked for an explanation. None was forthcoming. None the less, Hill flew the following day to the South of France to take part in a two-day test with the Williams team where he spoke with Frank Williams again.

For whatever motive, perhaps because Hill might have lowered his price, Williams admitted that the decision had 'nothing to do with money'. If that were the case, it was either a comment on Hill's driving or because another driver could bring something extra to the party.

Hill set the fastest time as if to prove a point, and flew home again. On Friday evening, Breen called a group of regular Formula One journalists to a meeting in London on the following Sunday morning. That triggered a stream of speculative stories for Saturday morning, suggesting that Hill's future was in the balance and the Sunday newspapers followed on suggesting everything from 'Hill Quits' to 'Hill Stays'. The truth emerged when Breen, now faced with a battery of television and radio crews and a much larger media audience than expected, revealed the situation. Hill stayed at home in Dublin. Breen read a prepared statement and went on to say that he 'would not be 100 per cent surprised' if Williams rang to have further talks.

Yet even as Breen was driving home from the Conrad Hotel in London, Frank Williams, having heard the news bulletins, cleared up the situation unequivocally by announcing: 'I can confirm that the Rothmans Williams Renault team will not be using Damon Hill's services in 1997.

'His replacement will be made known in due course.'

It was short, to the point, and cleared the way for a waterfall of speculation about his successor and where he might go and it completely severed any final hope Hill had although his lawyer was already in discussions with several other teams before the statement. The suspicion in the Hill camp was that Williams did not have a deal to do because he had already agreed terms with another driver, Heinz-Harald Frentzen, driving for the Sauber Ford team. Instead of giving Hill a rise

170

on his £4.5 million a year salary, he would probably pay half as much.

'We have no confirmation whether or not another driver has or had already been signed,' said Breen. 'It just seems very odd that the negotiations were so short and ended so abruptly. It could not have been about money for we never really got that far down the road. I would suggest that you could draw your own conclusions and speak to Frank Williams.

'We only began negotiations in mid-August and there were several points on the table but on Wednesday, 28 August, Frank called me at my office to withdraw from discussing Damon's contract any further. He gave no reason for his decision. Needless to say, Damon and I were very disappointed and surprised by the news. He would very much have liked the chance to go on and work with Williams and hopefully defend the title in the same car next season.

'Damon was very keen to drive for Williams. He's been there six years. Why would he not want to continue?'

Hill was following in the footsteps of Nigel Mansell who won the 1992 world title with Williams only to be called two days after the clinching win in Hungary to be told that his contract offer had been withdrawn.

Williams also contributed greatly to Alain Prost's decision to retire in 1993 after he won the world title for the fourth time, when he told him he had signed his bitter rival, Ayrton Senna, as his partner the following year. No one believed that Prost would drive with Senna or that the team could afford their massive salaries and Prost quit.

Breen claimed that in the 1995 negotiations for the coming season, they had pushed for a two-year deal but Frank Williams had refused, insisting that he had taken so much flak from sponsors and others in the past when he had not held onto his world champions.

'He told me exactly "let's wait and see what happens" when we both agreed a one-year deal for 1996,' said Breen. 'Then he added "I have already lost enough world champions and been berated by my sponsors and I never want that to happen again." Now it has, through no fault of ours.

'We were led to believe all the while that they were interested in Damon. There was no hint. It was a bolt from the blue. I called Damon to tell him and he was shocked.'

With a rueful smile, Breen agreed that the timing was 'not ideal' with three races still to go. Hill had a 13-point lead on the only man who could rob him of the title, his team-mate Villeneuve who had beaten him in the last two races in Hungary and Belgium. Hill needed to win the Italian Grand Prix, and Villeneuve not be in the top three, to be world champion after two years as runner-up.

'Damon was fastest in testing after hearing this news and is training at home and focusing on winning in Monza,' said Breen. 'He is upbeat. I am confident that Frank will continue to give the drivers equal equipment and ensure fair play... and no doubt people will be watching closely.'

He could not say which teams were interested in Hill but it was easy to identify those who needed a man with such vast experience. McLaren, Jordan and the new Jackie Stewart team were the likely bidders and although his price had been affected by the Williams announcement, he would have added value if he took with him the number one on his car next season.

'Discussions are underway to find the most attractive "fit" where he will be both happy and appreciated,' confirmed Breen. 'That is very important. It is not simply about money for Damon.'

Hill's name figured large on every mode of the media over the next few days but he sat quietly in Dublin while the speculation grew about Frentzen, not named by Williams who had taken another public pounding for lack of sensitivity, lack of respect and shortage of loyalty. Williams declined all requests for interviews but on Wednesday, as the drivers were preparing to leave for Monza, he finally released the worst kept secret in the sport by way of a simple statement which finally paid credit to Hill.

'German driver Heinz-Harald Frentzen will be joining the Rothmans Williams Renault team for 1997 alongside Canadian,

Jacques Villeneuve, who will be in his second year of a two-year contract.'

Twenty-nine-year-old Heinz-Harald would be replacing Damon Hill in the team, and when announcing his signing, team director Frank Williams paid tribute to the British world championship leader.

'Damon has contributed greatly to the team both as a test and race driver – he has done an excellent job for us. I think his record speaks for itself, as very few drivers have ever approached his record of 20 wins in 64 starts. He will be missed by everyone at our Grove factory and we all wish him the best of luck for the remainder of this year, as well as in the future.

'Heinz-Harald has been in Grand Prix racing since 1994 with Peter Sauber's Swiss-based team and prior to that he made his name as a member of the Mercedes-Benz junior team alongside Michael Schumacher and Karl Wendlinger.'

In Monza, Hill finally spoke for the first time, holding court in a marquee in mid-afternoon as a huge international media pack, hungry for every detail, swarmed around. He chose his words carefully but there was a feeling of frustration and betrayal from a man who clearly felt that he had given his all and been treated shabbily.

'Yes, it was a shock,' he confessed. 'I have every reason to believe Frank was extremely happy with my driving all season.

'I have had my reactions from Frank this season and also from Patrick Head [the technical director] which made me believe they were not only impressed but astonished and extremely pleased with the way I was driving. Frank was obviously very uncomfortable when he phoned me with the news but he had made his decision.'

'I thought the fact that I was leading the championship and had won seven races was something of an ace up my sleeve but you cannot count on anything.

'I was disappointed in his decision. I believe I turned myself round during the winter as a driver. I made myself the leading driver, I was leading the championship in my best season. My view was that the reward for winning regularly should be the chance to drive the best equipment.

'It is very easy to look back and say that some things were foretold. I did read a quote from Nigel Mansell's book where it actually comments on what may happen with Williams and myself, but, again, my view was that if I performed well enough and if I won races, I would be rewarded. You can say that is naive but it is the method I used to get into Formula One and that method to get the drive for this year.'

Hill said that Williams insisted his sacking was not about money although it was believed he was looking for a £3 million increase. 'I did ask Frank for reasons but I am not prepared to disclose what he told me.'

The Hill camp's theory was that Williams, looking for a new engine supplier for 1998 after the withdrawal of Renault from the sport, replaced Hill with Germany's Heinz-Harald Frentzen as part of a deal to secure engines from Munich-based BMW.

Hill might have been fifth and second in the last two races, his job taken away, but he was still defiant and confident about his future.

'Maybe it was time I left the nest after six years. This has opened options to explore with other teams who want my expertise to develop a winning car. In some ways this relieves the pressure. I knew when I went testing last week and set the fastest time. It made no difference.

'There is no reason for my relationship with Jacques to change. We get on fine but I believe I am a quicker driver and I believe I will beat him.'

Hill immediately went to the Williams pits when he arrived at the track and was given a good welcome and their support. Suggestions that the team might favour Villeneuve to help him win the title and keep the number one on a Williams car next season were rejected by Hill.

'I have had assurance from Frank and Patrick that I will be given equal treatment and equipment and I believe that to be true.'

Negotiations had started with several teams, he confirmed,

but he was in no hurry to sign. The name Ferrari emerged and Hill said he knew nothing of that but, as is the way of F1, did not rule it out, admitting: 'I would certainly not disregard Ferrari. Any driver in Formula One has a passion about Ferrari, they have a certain thing no one else has.'

That seemed the most unlikely move for it would team him with Michael Schumacher and if Hill carried the number one on the car, it could prove difficult. Still, it would be great box-office and that has a habit of making the seemingly impossible come true in F1.

Frentzen sat in the crowded Sauber Ford motor home and talked about the move he thought he might have missed when he turned down Frank Williams in 1994. That in itself was news for it emerged that Williams had tried to recruit Frentzen before elevating Scotsman David Coulthard to the seat from the test driving position.

'I told Frank that I could not join because Peter Sauber had given me my chance in Formula One again and I could not do it with a clear conscience. Some people thought I was stupid because I did not change teams and did not use the opportunity but I had to fix it with my conscience. We kept in touch since then, and after the race at Spa-Francorchamps, he told me that I had a very good chance to drive for Williams next year.'

He was quizzed on whether he had signed a deal months earlier but said that only an option existed on his services which many drivers have with other teams as they cover themselves for loss of form, accidents or simply look to change for the future.

There was much talk of Frentzen's relations with Schumacher, for he was once rated much more highly than the world champion and the two had also tangled off track when his girlfriend, Corinna, had departed to the arms of the man who would be king, and became his wife.

'I think Frank Williams has signed me because he wants me to beat Michael next year,' said Frentzen in reply to questioning about his ability to cope with the challenge. 'I think I can beat him otherwise I would not be the right man.

'It is hard to believe I have signed. It will take time to sink in. So far I have not had time to open champagne, just a beer.

'I always rated Damon as a very good driver and I wish him well for the rest of the season.'

Hill, who believed he would have a 'professional' relationship with Williams for the rest of the season, said: 'It's been fair to say I feel like I have been to Mars and back in the last ten days. There has been so much to-ing and fro-ing. It was a shock and disappointing. But I have had worse shocks in life and F1 and I will get over this one and continue to press on and to get results.'

If he were a team manager why would he hire himself? 'I am not going to sit here and sell myself,' he said and then promptly did so with some aplomb.

'It is true to say that I have had a considerable input to the performance of the team and also to the development of the car, not only this car but other cars at Williams. I consider myself to be one of the best in the business at producing a car that is competitive in all situations.

'Teams are always interested in developing their cars and I am looking to drive the most competitive car. It has to be the right total package. It is not sufficient to simply take on a project. I want to win and get results and if I can go to a team and the right ingredients are there to make the step forward from not being a winning team to winning, then that would be my choice.

'I am not a quitter. I am looking for the right package which would allow me to utilise all my talents to make them a winning team. I will press on and get results. My goal is winning the championship and this gives me extra motivation.'

By Friday, speculation was rife that Hill's bid for a top drive next season was being boosted by Formula One power-broker Bernie Ecclestone and Jean Alesi's mouth. Hill, dumped by Williams, was virtually invited to join the Jordan team, but as he prepared for the Italian Grand Prix, the possibility of a move to Benetton began to emerge.

Ecclestone, the president of the Formula One Constructors Association, was keen to keep Hill in a competitive car to keep the battles tight at the front end next year and said: 'I want to see Damon in a top car next season. It would be a loss if he was not.'

Benetton's drivers, Gerhard Berger and Alesi were contracted until the end of 1997 but the team had been having a dismal season after winning everything with Michael Schumacher last season. Alesi, a fiery Frenchman, launched a scathing attack on the team which had strained his relations with them and the Italian press believed this could lead to an early departure.

'I want to be a racing driver, not a taxi driver,' said Alesi. 'With this car I lose all possibility of showing what I can do. The car has a lot of problems. It's not normal that the Williams car, with the same Renault engine, is much faster than us.

'My aim at the start of the season was much different to what has happened. I am here competing at the end of the championship for a lowly place in the final classification. I started with big ambitions but again I will have to wait until the next championship.'

That brought a curt response from Benetton boss, Flavio Briatore: 'He would be better off watching Berger's times and shutting up.'

Briatore was at his most cryptic when asked if he would be interested in Hill.

'Yes and no,' replied the Italian. To the question of whether Alesi would be driving for Benetton next year, he said: 'I never believe anything in Formula One.'

He had earlier denied that Alesi would leave the team but he is right: in F1, anything is possible and especially with Ecclestone keen to keep the interest high as ITV take over from BBC with a £70 million contract. Williams running with a Canadian and a German and Benetton with a Frenchman and an Austrian, while Eddie Irvine was well down the pecking order at Ferrari as Schumacher's assistant, did little to stir British blood. The problem with the Hill for McLaren theory was that David Coulthard was definitely there for 1997 and that would mean two British drivers in a team which would have huge German backing from Mercedes and West cigarettes.

McLaren boss Ron Dennis was still looking for 'the best available driver' and Eddie Jordan said in Monza: 'I would be delighted to have Damon. He would be a great asset. He is fantastically professional and it would be boost for Jordan if he came to us.'

Yet his team was again failing to live up to its promise and Hill running at six or seven would be less than ideal, particularly if he had number one on his car.

Business as Usual

Hill spun off in the morning session of free practice and finished the day seventh over the two-hour sessions, Schumacher was top, confirming Ferrari's potential, Villeneuve was a frustrated fifth, Alesi sixth and Frentzen eighth. All four men figured large in Hill's life but he was a picture of happiness, insisting that he had more motivation from the past few days and that he was unaffected – 'not one bit, not an iota'.

'The times are not representative of what our true potential is,' he said with a smile.

'Happy to be back in action? You bet. I would rather drive than talk – and you will probably agree with that.

'There is no difference in team atmosphere. I have had a lot of good reaction and support. It's business as usual. I feel every bit as confident as I have ever done. I feel more motivated than ever. The decision has not affected me. Not really. Once you are in the car you don't have time to think about contracts or anything. You are just positioning the car and opening the throttle.

'I have not seen Frank yet. I really have not had a chance.'

He confirmed that his engineering would be done with Adrian Newey and Ian Preston 'as usual' with input from technical director Patrick Head 'as usual'. He threw no light on contract talks and although Breen was at the race, they insisted they would not strike any deals until the outcome of the title was decided, which also allowed Ecclestone time to use his own powers of persuasion if he so chose.

Schumacher was in sprightly mood and when the subject of Hill came up, he refused to say whether he thought Williams would be stronger without his rival but said: 'I will not answer for it would be good for Frentzen and bad for Damon.'

He added: 'We always talk about Damon's wins and some people, me included, think "how good is he?" Does the car win races or is it him? By changing to another team we are going to see what he is really like and it will be an opportunity for him to prove he is better than some people think.

It might be, some will get a surprise and we will know his ability and how good is the car, how good he is himself.'

Hill had forecast that qualifying on Saturday would be thrilling, the closest of the season and the crowds rolled into Monza in their usual traffic-stopping thousands. The atmosphere at Monza is electric, raucous, full of anticipation, fun and Ferrari. The *tifosi*, the fanatics who worship at the shrine of the Prancing Horse, flood the park, a beautiful haven of peace and picnics for most of the year until September when it comes alive like a sleeping monster.

The circuit, built in 1922, no longer has the old bankings although some are still visible, but early in the morning, as you stand and watch the sun rise to burn away the dawn chill, it is possible to imagine the sights and sounds of days gone by, to conjure up visions of Nuvolari, Fangio, Ascari, Hawthorn, Stewart, Senna.

Outside the paddock, a cauldron of rumour, tittle-tattle and fact at this time of year, a crowd of fans gaze through the railings hoping for a glimpse of anyone famous, screaming with delight if a driver appears. Thankfully, some drivers do go forward and sign autographs, some throw caps and badges over the fence. Disgracefully, this year, someone, although no one owned up, had ordered sacking to be hung over the railings to cover the 30 yards of viewing area. It did not last long as the eager hands hauled down the curtain but it indicated a crassness beyond belief in an official mind. More than 13,000 had turned up to watch Schumacher's test session a week earlier at Monza and that sort of support has to be nourished.

They come on bikes and scooters, in Ferraris and old Fiats and they carry flags of all the drivers, banners proclaiming everything from, 'Look up to the sky, Gerhard, it is the only thing greater than you' to even 'Montermini – keep believing'. There were also many Union Jacks and a few banners for Hill, one insisting stridently: 'Damon – you will be world champion this year.'

Hill's attitude was just as confident and his performance in a qualifying session which failed to live up to its billing was equally as satisfying. For almost 30 minutes the only thing that moved was the sun in the sky as the teams waited to see who would move first and tried to protect tyres which suffer on the high-speed circuit. Eventually it was Jacques Villeneuve who went out for 6 laps, indicating that most would do just two runs. Hill ventured out and seemed unable to match his team-mate's time until his sixth lap when suddenly he went top, 0.136th of a second faster.

A massive roar erupted as Schumacher's first split time showed him fastest but there was only muted encouragement when he came in second.

With 6 minutes to go, Hill was out again and Schumacher was right behind. Again, Hill wound it up and on the ninth lap went just over half a second fastest, 0.577 of a second, on 1 minute 24.204 for the 3.6 miles round the park. Villeneuve pushed hard to get up to second but Schumacher had to settle for third having done only 9 of his 12 available laps.

'Obviously I have not lost the knack of going quickly and that is a relief,' said Hill pointedly. 'It is particularly satisfying for a number of reasons to be on pole . . . and I think you all know what they are. I have not lost anything as a driver and I have performed well all weekend.

'I think I am still as quick as ever I was and I have performed as well here today as I have performed all season.'

Was there any possibility of a non-aggression pact between himself and Villeneuve for the start to avoid a collision at the first corner?

'It would be a pretty pointless conversation, I would have thought,' said Hill. 'There is going to be a fight tomorrow to win the race.'

Villeneuve, who had had a bad crash which he stepped out of in the morning warm-up after Pedro Diniz came across him, called the Brazilian 'one of those idiot drivers who should not be in F1' and was unhappy with his car set-up. (Diniz was absolved of blame by the stewards.) He was also disgruntled about the kerbs at the two chicanes, saying that they had to be hit hard to keep the line. The high kerbs of previous years had been replaced by lower concrete structures which could be driven over. Three short, fixed tyre walls, three tyres high, had been erected on the inside of each apex to top cars cutting the corners after it was obvious that plastic bollards were just being knocked out. Those coming later were simply slicing over the apexes but Villeneuve's car had kicked up a concrete section and the danger was obvious.

Hill explained: 'Jacques, Gerhard and myself were called to canvass opinion among drivers and we all agreed that something had to be done. How do you legislate for what is unfair?

'The tyres are not the perfect solution but they are better than nothing. This morning Jacques went over a kerb where a car had pulled out a great lump of concrete and the whole kerb is made up of concrete teeth and it just does not bear thinking about what could happen.

'The best thing is to keep everyone off the kerb and tyres are a good solution, a temporary one. You don't want to hit the tyres, though, that is the problem.'

Those words were absoutely prophetic a day later.

Tyred and Emotional

Sunday dawned with talk of the big event: Hill was to meet actor Bruce Willis. Briefly, it took everyone's minds off the pressure situation. Sadly, Bruce stayed away and missed a great race.

Hill looked calm and relaxed and on the grid, 15 minutes before the start, he did what racing drivers do well and provided an interview for BBC's live programme. Try interviewing a footballer or rugby player minutes before a game and they freak out.

Villeneuve sat in his car, preferring the privacy of the cockpit. Schumacher got out and talked to those around, went for his usual trip to the toilet and returned to a cacophonous welcome.

The roar which split the clear blue sky about 20 minutes later was even greater, a long, deafening sound wave punctuated with whistles and klaxons, and Damon Hill put his hands to his helmet as if hoping for momentary deafness to match the lack of vision a few seconds earlier.

Hill and Villeneuve had wanted to see fair play and safety as they duelled in Italy for the world title but little did they know that they were also voting for their own downfall.

Michael Schumacher sparked a massive invasion with his win, a Ferrari red carpet, human flooring of *tifosi* but Hill and his rival had to make do with rubber matting which guided them to disappointment. Both Williams drivers had voted for the black tyre bollards to stop cars cutting the corner at the chicanes but they were victims of that decision.

As the noise engulfed Hill he was already sliding to a halt in his stricken car, for as he focused on the race he had lost sight of the very barrier he had asked for and ended a week of upheaval in the shadows. One moment he had been leading the race by 2.9 seconds after only 6 laps, the next he had clipped a tyre bollard and slid gracefully to a halt in the middle of the track in the shade of a bridge. The delighted pack raced past the stranded Williams car, Hill clambered out to safety and hung his head. It was not supposed to be like this, he thought. It should be: Hill wins, Jacques Villeneuve is not in the top three, Hill takes world title. Frank Williams, who had discarded Hill for next season a few days ago for Heinz-Harald Frentzen, would be embarrassed as the Englishman accepted the glory. All of this zipped through Hill's head.

Behind him, further up the track, past a soundbite from a

red-bedecked section of the 170,000 crowd, all Ferrari *tifosi*, men, women and children, who jeered and howled with delight, stood the dark, defiant tyres at the exit of the last part of a chicane. He did not know that the tyres would inflict a savage blow to Villeneuve which would enhance Hill's 13-point lead and send him off happier than he had any right to expect.

'We will just have to be careful,' Hill had said a day earlier. How those words must have haunted him and how Villeneuve, who struggled to finish seventh, must have wished he had come up with another solution, for he had said: 'The tyres are not a good solution for the race.' He clipped the tyres heavily and bent 'something' on the front of his Williams car and observed dolefully: 'The car changed completely. I did not have high top speed and in the opening laps I was nowhere down the straights.'

That incident accounted for more than just himself for David Coulthard was following close behind and the swaying tyres hit his front wheel and broke his steering, forcing him out.

Hill was smarting from his own error but admitted: 'I am a very lucky man indeed to escape with my lead in place. Jacques has not capitalised on the situation.

'I can offer no explanation for what happened other than I did not concentrate hard enough and it was my mistake.

'I was going great. I was having a stonking good race. I had made a great start and I was aggressive. Jean Alesi got the lead but I managed to get by. I was pushing beautifully and the car was really stretching its legs. Then I clipped the tyres and that yanked the steering wheel out of my hands and spun the car round. I hit the tyres hard enough to bend the suspension for they were bolted down.

'I cannot blame anyone for putting them there!

'At that stage I was not allowing myself to think about winning, I was just focusing on the race ahead. I am kicking myself for what happened. It is a race victory that I have lost. That is what really hurts most. I am disappointed for the team, for the guys who worked so hard. I have not been able to pay them back for their work.'

Hill had another fear when he stopped for he looked back and saw Alesi, who had made a brilliant start to move from third to first off the grid, only to lose it to a fiercely aggressive title favourite, bearing down on him.

'I was pretty worried,' he admitted. 'I was anxious to get out for I could see the cars coming down behind me and I just had to ditch the car. Then I went back to help the marshals move it.'

The tyres were relentless, enemies of at least ten drivers who dared to take them on. Hill might just manage a wry smile at finding that his replacement next season, Frentzen, lasted only two laps longer before hitting the tyres and spinning into the gravel.

That's how the day had started, with all the talk surrounding Frentzen, Hill, Villeneuve. Schumacher changed all that. On the day that he announced that his wife Corinna was four months pregnant with their first child, the world champion gave new life to the Ferrari dream in their own backyard. They had not celebrated the Prancing Horse's gallop to the chequered flag at Monza, a historic, proud, emotive circuit which encourages high speed and even greater courage, since 1988 when Gerhard Berger won.

There had been a little reluctance to accept Schumacher in a mixed season for the team but the £1 million-a-race man really delivered a massive return on investment on that Sunday. He hounded Jean Alesi until the Benetton man departed for an earlier pit-stop. Schumacher pushed on to build up a lead and was in and out with fresh tyres and fuel to retain that advantage until the delirious end of the 53-lap race.

The fans exploded on the track, a sea of red, the parties started and Schumacher could only marvel at what he had released.

'Fantastic, just fantastic,' he said. 'I have goosebumps all over my body. They deserve this for they have waited so long. I had one anxious moment when I hit the tyre barrier hard but I was lucky.'

Hill had also been extremely lucky, he had got out of jail free and now his position had improved for Villeneuve had to beat him by four points or better at the next race in Portugal to prevent the coronation.

'I will try to keep the pressure on and hope he makes another mistake,' said Villeneuve as Hill sentenced himelf to 48 hours hard labour by going to Austria to the home of his trainer, Erwin Gollner, to work out. Then he took on a one-day test at the A1 circuit, as the Österreichring was now called, with the Williams team. There was to be no let up, no respite in his preparations. There could be no more errors.

At least he left with another ringing recommendation from Ecclestone who said: 'It seems Frank Williams does not like world champions in the team. He makes them and then gets rid of them. Damon should be in a top team. He is a much better driver this season.'

Race 14: Italian Grand Prix

Result	Drivers (overall)	Constructors (overall)
1. Michael Schumacher (Ger)	1. Hill 81	1. Williams 149
2. Jean Alesi (Fra)	2. Villeneuve 68	2. Benetton 61
3. Mika Hakkinen (Fin)	3. Schumacher 49	3. Ferrari 58
4. Martin Brundle (GB)		
5. Rubens Barrichello (Bra)		
6. Pedro Diniz (Bra)		

16

Party Time – For Jacques

Portuguese Grand Prix, Estoril: 22 September

Hill brought his guitar and a veiled warning for rival Jacques Villeneuve when he arrived at the Estoril circuit on 19 September, feeling very at home on a track where Williams do much of their test work in the winter.

The attendant international media, mainly British augmented by Germans, French, Brazilians, Italians and Japanese, sat him down in the congested dining area under the awning attached to the Williams motor home and began interrogation. As usual, it was a mix of banter and questioning about his current state of mind, his confidence, track conditions, fitness, attitude to his team-mate, off-track activities, relationship with Frank Williams and his employment prospects. There were big pressures on Hill but he sat on a stool, holding a microphone, and tried to give a good impression of a relaxed, cool customer.

Interest was high for this seemed to be the place where he would hit the jackpot, the last of the European races, the perfect, sociable town, the ideal track.

Hill had flown to Austria immediately after Italy to work on his fitness but most of the gap between races had been at home, with his family and awaiting news of future employment. His determination to be fit to fight to the end had taken him away with team trainer Erwin Gollner who lives near Salzburg.

'It was just good to get out of the gym at home,' said Hill. 'That can get a bit monotonous. You start to feel like a laboratory rat working in there. We had two good days of training.'

Hill had also joined up with the Williams team for a test session at the A1 track, previously the Österreichring, last used for the Austrian Grand Prix in 1987 and now due to return in revamped form in 1997.

Yes, there had also been lots of discussions and phone calls about his future employment. No, he could not throw any light on those because things were confidential. So, what was to be his approach to a race where he needed to finish ahead of his team-mate to take the title? Softly, softly or aggressive win-racing stuff?

'There are a lot of things to look at,' said Hill. 'My aim is to win. I made a mistake at Monza. The things which go through your mind in the heat of the race are those things which determine your mode of driving. I made a very aggressive start and then decided to drive more cautiously.'

It transpired that Hill, contrary to public opinion which had wondered why he had not just taken it easy going through the tricky tyre barrier-protected chicane, had done just that and lost a touch of concentration in the act.

'I feel quite relaxed, my nerves are not jangling as some people would have you believe,' he said pointedly. 'I know Estoril like the back of my hand. I have tested here for years and it is an excellent circuit. It is also one of the most dangerous on the calendar. There is not enough run-off area at some corners and it is bumpy, difficult to drive, but I like it from that aspect.

'There is a kilometre-long straight, a fantastic 180 degree last corner where you can be pulling four G for five or six seconds, some overtaking points and it is very physical. I am looking forward to it.

'You need to be aggressive. To do a quick lap you need a blend of finesse and aggression. I have always aimed to win races and that has not changed.'

Yet in his words there seemed to be a hint of compromise with this approach. After the first lap, he said, he would take time to consider his position. He would take all the per-mutations in his head and then work out what was required. In other words, despite aiming to win, if he found Villeneuve back down the field, he could afford to ease up and just stay ahead. His French-Canadian team-mate had to beat him on

Sunday in the Portuguese Grand Prix to extend the title race to the final round in Japan and although the Williams drivers continued their public friendship, the tensions were building underneath.

Villeneuve had been quoted in the French newspaper *Le Monde* days earlier talking about Hill on track manners and had said: 'This season Damon has blocked me many times at the start. In Australia when I was on pole I did not try to squeeze him. I went straight. I have come to understand that he does not do the same thing.

'It is all too easy to zigzag at the start and then say that after that I got a little sideways. We are Formula One drivers and should be capable of controlling the car in a straight line.

'I do not know if I am ready to do the same thing myself. It is very hard to get someone on the grass or block them deliberately but I would not feel bad to do it to Damon because he has done it to me so many times this season.'

Hill was tackled on that but merely raised his eyebrows and smiled. There was no problem between himself and Villeneuve he insisted, and that did appear to be the case during the weekend. He was asked about comments made in several magazines by drivers past and present about what he should do to win the title, with several suggesting, only semi-jokingly, that he should drive Villeneuve off the track.

If neither man scored points, Hill would be champion. It was not exactly a radical suggestion in Formula One. Had not Michael Schumacher driven into Hill in 1994 in Adelaide in the final race when he was crashing out and being overtaken by the Englishman, who would have won the title if he had finished? Instead, Hill's car was damaged by Schumacher's wrecked Benetton which had hit a wall seconds before Hill came round a corner and Schumacher won the title by a single point.

Alain Prost and his bitter rival, his team-mate at McLaren, Ayrton Senna, had traded similar incidents in world title deciders, and in the heat of battle as cars raced into corners at high speed, particularly in a bunched start, the stewards often found it impossible or were unwilling to apportion blame.

Hill shook his head. 'Let me make it clear that I do not want to resort to unfair tactics,' he said. 'I am against them and I have seen championships won in a way which I think was unsatisfactory. I clearly feel that I can win the championship on merit and driving performance. There are all sorts of views about how drivers should conduct themselves.'

The questioning on that line continued as some tried to find hidden meaning in his remarks or simply sought to clarify what he meant. Having cleared that up, he then reacted curiously when asked if that meant he would not deliberately drive Villeneuve off the track to secure the title for himself.

'Wouldn't I?' replied Hill. 'What I am saying is that anything is possible. It is always a matter of opinion what is fair. I drive the way I feel fit at a given time and I am at liberty to drive in a way that may not be the way people expect me to drive.

'I have everything at my disposal. I don't always have to give way. I will defend vigorously if I am in the lead.'

Hill is one of the gentlemen of the circuit, not in a prissy way, but more as a decent bloke, slightly introverted, and accusations of him being too nice are overplayed. The message he seemed to be sending was clear – he would do what was necessary to the limit of the law to win the title.

Now to God. Hill had crashed when leading early in Italy but watched with relief as Michael Schumacher won for Ferrari while Villeneuve finished outside the points.

'Monza proved two things,' said Hill with a smile. 'God is on the side of Ferrari and he wants me to win the championship. To knock myself out of the race and not lose my points advantage was something of a miracle.'

The Italian press, always a seething hotbed of rumour and speculation for a public who love motorsport, claimed that Hill would sign for Jordan on the Monday following the race. Jordan signed Ralf Schumacher, 21-year-old brother of Michael, for 1997 and produced him at a press conference on Friday morning.

No, said Hill, he would not be signing, and everyone went off happy. Journalists to write their stories, and Hill, who had a group of friends and his wife Georgie at the race, to strum a guitar in the motor home and have a laugh before starting work with his engineers on race set-up.

That night, however, events took a different turn when a group of British journalists met up with Bernie Ecclestone, the diminutive figure who runs Formula One from his offices in London or from inside the smoked glass grey motor home that is his office at races. Ecclestone, apart from being worth over £100 million, is the powerbroker of F1, a straight-to-the-point man who has fought his way to the top, knows the business inside out and has more strings in his hand than a balloon trader in Covent Garden.

He is a fan of Hill, a fan of the show, but his message was pretty stark: Hill should consider retiring or accept that he would have to join a team that gave him no chance of the world title in 1997. Ecclestone also believed that Hill would have to take a massive pay-cut just to stay in the sport, dropping his wages by as much as £3 million.

The winner of 20 races in his short career at the top, Hill had hoped that McLaren or Benetton would move in for his services after Williams dropped him. McLaren had now re-signed Mika Hakkinen and it emerged that Jean Alesi, the Benetton driver who might have been asked to depart his contract a year early, was asking £12 million for a buy-out, a straight message saying: 'I am staying.'

Eddie Irvine had not set anything on fire at Ferrari as Schumacher's sidekick but there was no real chance that they would replace him with a direct rival for Schumacher around whom the team was being built. That left the middle teams, and perhaps to help Hill make his mind up and face reality, Ecclestone indicated that only fifth-ranked Jordan or the new Jackie Stewart team could be in the hunt although the Ligier team, owned by Flavio Briatore, another Hill fan, were also interested.

Eddie Jordan was desperate to have Hill team up with

Schumacher junior. Hill would bring the world champion number one to his car, for his speed and his skill in developing a car. Jackie Stewart, three times world champion, now coming back with his own team, had a five-year engine deal with Ford, and at the launch of a five-year £25 million sponsorship deal with the Hongkong and Shanghai Banking Corporation a week earlier, he had declared: 'We would love to recruit Damon. He has tremendous skills and talents and I think he is mature and well balanced.'

Ecclestone put it on the line. 'He should seriously consider quitting. He does not have many options. He is going to have to quit or give something back to the sport. You've got to know when to go, when you have peaked, and then you say adios.

'He might have to retire. It is unfortunate he cannot defend the championship in the team he is likely to win the championship with but Frank does not want him.

'If he went to Jordan he would not be able to defend his championship but if he accepted that, it would be bloody good for him and the sport. He would be doing the sport a great service. If he is not in a position to defend his title, this is the next best thing he could do.

'If he went to Jordan, he would be sacrificing his chances but he could say "I am happy and I will help the team and [Ralf] Schumacher and give something to the sport." '

Hill said: 'I have not considered retiring but I am not going to reveal what my plans are. If I win the world championship, I will have achieved the ultimate goal in Formula One – that has always been my aim.'

He had had talks with McLaren boss Ron Dennis and Benetton's Flavio Briatore but Ecclestone said: 'Ron does not want him and Flavio would take him but cannot.'

Michael Breen, Hill's experienced lawyer, scorned the notion that they had asked for £10 million from Williams, insisting: 'There seems to be some idea being put around that I am a novice at negotiations. I spend my life doing these kinds of contracts and I have been working successfully with Damon for six years.

'We are not stupid. We tried to negotiate with Frank Williams but we never got as far as money. He himself said it was nothing to do with money and that has not changed.'

Very Exciting

Hill shrugged it all off and went on to the practice session to emerge content with second fastest time of the day, Villeneuve fifth. Schumacher was fastest but worrying that the track did not suit Ferrari as it wrecked their tyres faster.

Hill appeared at the Friday Five inquisition and was asked about having two Schumachers on the grid in 1997. He laughed and replied: 'At one point I thought the world could bear only one Schumacher. Now we have two and it is going to be fascinating.

'Until this year I did not even know he had a brother so it has all caught me by surprise. He seems very confident and has a great opportunity coming into F1 with a team like Jordan.'

He made no reference to the possibility of driving with Schumacher if he accepted Jordan's offer.

The Saturday qualifying session was a hot one. Eight minutes into the session, Hill took over the lead from Irvine and on his second run of 3 laps improved to 1 minute 20.330 seconds for the 2.7 mile circuit. That put him almost a second ahead of everyone and even when Schumacher forced his way up to second, he was still nine-tenths of a second behind.

Alesi improved to second but with 15 minutes to go, Villeneuve ventured out and was flying. His split times were better but when he hit the line, he had failed to beat Hill by 9000ths of a second.

'Very exciting, great,' declared Hill. 'Very disappointing, frustrating,' said Villeneuve.

'It would be nice to get it all over here tomorrow,' said Hill who then covered all eventualities by saying: 'I don't mind if it goes to Japan.'

Villeneuve got in his little dig that he normally beat Damon at the start and hoped it would be the same this time – not quite as it turned out.

Aggressive Start

Just over 24 hours later, someone had cut Jacques out of the celebration cake which bore two little cars and an iced message offering good wishes. It sat in the Williams motor home but it was definitely not Damon who had done the cutting either on or off the track. The mystery guest who had sliced the cake bearing Hill's rival's name would have found it easier to swallow than the unpalatable truth choking Hill that he had been beaten, outpaced, outmanoeuvred by his world title rival, forcing him to take their duel to the final race in Suzuka.

Hill expected to emerge from his car at the end of the Portuguese Grand Prix wearing the mark of respectability as world champion but it was the old question mark about his speed which stayed over him as the huddled groups in the paddock discussed his latest failure to clinch the title.

Honourably, Hill was the first to admit: 'He did a great job of coming from fourth to win here. It is no mean feat. When he got in front, I tried to stay with him but Jacques was too quick. He was flying and I could not keep up with him.'

That view concurred with similar thoughts from Patrick Head, the Williams technical director, who insisted that by the time a clutch problem had materialised, Hill had been outpaced.

'I don't believe the clutch cost him the race,' said Head. 'By the time there were any signs of the problem, Jacques was already well ahead. When we told Damon, he was 6 seconds behind Villeneuve. Jacques had long gone. He won the race on speed which Damon did not have. He lost a lot of time in the middle of the race and I do not know why.'

Hill's hand seemed to stretch for the title when he went 13.5 seconds ahead of his closest chaser, Alesi, whom he had muscled out with an aggressive start as he held off the Benetton and Villeneuve. On lap 16 he was 15.6 seconds clear of

Villeneuve who was in fourth place behind Schumacher.

The engraver must have been poised to work on putting D.D. Hill on the old trophy but 54 laps later, the same man trailed in as a runner-up, 19.9 seconds behind, to the disbelief of many, including some of his own team.

Two incidents summed up the changing fortunes and perhaps the attitudes of both men. As Hill enjoyed his soft cushion of time on lap 16, Villeneuve, being held up by Schumacher, suddenly made an audacious move which he had talked about with his pit crew before the race.

Coming up to lap a Minardi, Schumacher eased slightly, looked in his mirror and found Villeneuve was missing. The 25-year-old French-Canadian had outsmarted him by going on the outside of the final corner coming into the long pit straight to overtake, a most unusual and risky move. He held his car, his line and his nerve to squeeze past the Ferrari and get inside the Minardi and was up to third and could now chase very hard.

'It was worth it to take the risk,' said Villeneuve who was lauded for the daring manoeuvre. 'I had nothing to lose. If I did not do it, I knew Damon would be world champion.

'It was fun overtaking on the outside on the last turn. I told the team before the race that I was sure I could do it. They said they would pick me off the guard-rail.'

Schumacher was also impressed. 'Suddenly he was alongside me and it was a little bit dangerous for his wheel was in between my front and back wheels and I could not slow down and he was in front.'

There still seemed little danger to Hill's lead and although after the first round of pit-stops it was down to a fraction under 10 seconds on the 28th lap, it suddenly began to evaporate in the warmest weather the old town of Estoril could provide during the weekend.

By the time he emerged after his stop on lap 34, Hill had a 7 second lead. Villeneuve headed for tyres and fuel 1 lap later and then mounted a supercharged attack on the Englishman. Within 2 laps, he was in Hill's mirrors, and 2 laps after that, he was right on his exhaust pipes. It was Hill's undoing for he pitted for the third and final time on lap 49 and was at a halt for 8.8 seconds. Villeneuve pitted on the 50th lap, halted for 8 seconds and that fraction of a second saved by his crew, and Hill's lack of top speed on that circuit, saw him emerge from the pitlane in front, to Damon's dismay.

'I saw a car coming out and thought it was a Tyrrell or something,' said Hill. 'I was just hoping it would get out of the way and then I saw the name Rothmans on the rear wing. I was pretty shocked but he was really going for it.

'I knew I just had to get down to it but I was unable to keep up. Then I got a warning about the clutch at about 16 laps from the end. The alarm bells were ringing for, after what happened in Monza, I was determined not to throw away more points and I decided to slow down. I decided it was best if I kept the loss of points to the minimum.'

Head confirmed that Hill had not been advised to slow down and he had made changes to the clutch himself with the aid of the in-car electronics which helped the problem.

'I felt Damon should have wrapped up the championship here,' said Head, 'but I still expect him to win in Japan. I would bet on that.'

Hill's delays were mystifying but he explained: 'I had to slow down because an Arrows and a Minardi were racing each other and were all over the road and not looking in their mirrors. That cost a few seconds on that lap.'

Perhaps he should have pushed on but he said: 'I had no way of knowing what the ultimate effects would be on the clutch and I wanted to get to the end.'

Yet it could all have been so different but for David Coulthard. For the Scot, who had been bizarrely bumped off the track by his own feuding team-mate Hakkinen, had been on the way back to the pits slowly when Hill came upon him and was delayed.

Then, after a quick stop, Hill was poised to leave when Coulthard came struggling down the pitlane and the Williams man with the stop–go lollipop board had no option but to delay departure. It may only have cost a second but consider that Villeneuve was probably only half a second at most ahead when he emerged in front of Hill from his pit-stop a lap later. Even Villeneuve, whose stop was 8 seconds compared to Hill's 8.8 seconds, admitted that one second longer made all the difference.

Hill put a brave face on things. 'I cannot be too disappointed. I am just one point away from the world championship. Jacques has to win and I only need to finish in the top six.

'My odds are better now than before the race. I am in a stronger position than I was. I have waited all season for the title, longer than that even, and I can wait until Suzuka.'

Villeneuve was as feisty as ever. 'Anything can happen in motor-racing. It will be tough but we will see how it goes. It is not over until the chequered flag.'

The Williams team stayed on with most others to continue testing but Hill, not required until mid-week, opted to fly home to see his family in Dublin before returning on Wednesday.

Teams interested in his services had also been invited to tender sealed bids and complete a small questionnaire about the package being offered. His eyes were on the future but many outsiders, and a few inside, were now wondering if the Fates had turned against Hill. Were we on the verge of a great British sporting disaster?

Race 15: Portuguese Grand Prix

Result	Drivers (overall)	Constructors (overall)
1. Jacques Villeneuve (Can)	1. Hill 87	1. Williams 165
2. Damon Hill (GB)	2. Villeneuve 78	2. Benetton 65
3. Michael Schumacher (Ger)	3. Schumacher 53	3. Ferrari 64
4. Jean Alesi (Fra)		
5. Eddie Irvine (GB)		
6. Gerhard Berger (Aut)		

17

Glory Day

Japanese Grand Prix, Suzuka: 13 October

O n Thursday, 26 September, Damon, fresh from testing in
Estoril, took a drive into the rolling Oxfordshire country-
side but the only scenery on his mind was the view inside the
TWR factory at Leafield.

Hill had been contacted immediately after the Italian Grand
Prix by Tom Walkinshaw, who told him he was very interested
in his services once the driver was ready to talk business. Jordan
and Stewart Grand Prix were also very keen to have him but
no one suspected that Arrows, now owned by 50-year-old
Walkinshaw, would have a chance. After all, any team which
had a race-to-win ratio of 287 to zero hardly seemed attractive
to a man with 20 wins from 66 races, one of the best in the
history of the sport.

Hill toured the factory, was amazed at the facilities and after
a seven-hour visit decided to sign for a year. He was announced
the following day to an astonished motorsport world who
described the move as everything from 'joining the flops' to
shortsighted.

Hill was to be paid close to his existing £4.5 million salary
and he said: 'I chose Arrows because they offered me everything
I was looking for. It was the best package deal I could have
chosen.

'Tom fulfilled every criterion I set for myself. The opportunity
to make rapid progress with a team, test, develop – and the
carrot of winning races at the end of it all.'

The sceptics preyed heavily on the Arrows record and were helped by Jordan's disappointed commercial director, Ian Phillips, who went public with his thoughts to add to the perception that Hill had lost his appetite for hard work and had opted for the easier life, passing time with a team which was living to survive.

Arrows suspected things were going their way when Hill looked at the mould for the new monocoque and asked how much room there was for his feet. What size was he? asked car designer Frank Dernie. Hill replied: 'Eleven – so make sure there is enough room in there.'

The press and public were less convinced so, less than a week later, Walkinshaw threw open the doors of his factory to allow some media the chance to see what had attracted Hill. The little wooden shack which stands among the space-age buildings of Hill's new team headquarters was used by Scott of the Antarctic for radio signals to Britain, but Walkinshaw's message was more hopeful for his new driver's adventure in Formula One next season.

Walkinshaw offered the media the same guided tour of the £15 million base. 'The Arrows team you will see next year is not the one you have watched this year,' said the chunky Scot who has built up his empire in 20 years to a £250 million turnover. 'It is a totally new team.

'Damon thought he was leaving the first division with Williams for the third division but after he saw the facilities we have got here, he knew we had the tools to do the job.

'Next year we are looking to be in the top five, we expect several podium finishes and if we get that then we could get one or two Grand Prix wins. The following year we are looking at being in the top three as a team and we should be going head-to-head for the championship by 2000.'

No message has ever been spelled out clearer at the Leafield site, which began life as the base for Scott the explorer, was owned by Marconi and latterly was a British Telecom training and signal centre.

Walkinshaw took over the Arrows team in July. He revealed

that he had ordered his engineers and resources to be poured into the development of next year's car and had installed the latest equipment costing over £5 million to prepare for the new era. Hill was taken aback when he toured, not only by the technology but by the organisation and the size of the drawing office. He did not even talk about salary until he had made up his mind that TWR was the place for him, rejecting the higher-ranked Jordan team and the new Jackie Stewart outfit with topline Ford engines.

'He knows that to be at the top level, he needs to have these facilities, a state-of-the-art wind tunnel, research and development, the best testing equipment, all the things we have. What you see here does not come cheap.'

Walkinshaw built up the same standards of excellence when he joined the Benetton team, an ailing outfit in 1991, and as technical director helped them become world constructors' champions in 1994 when their driver, Michael Schumacher, won the world drivers' title, beating Hill.

'The Damon Hill you saw in 1996 is a far, far better driver than anything you have seen before,' he insisted. 'He's still hungry to win with us and he sees that possibility. Once he is on the podium he will smell the possibility to win again.'

They had agreed a one-year contract but Walkinshaw said that was only because the financial men became involved with a series of 'what ifs' and both parties decided to use a short-term deal as an incentive to deliver and then talk about a longer period deal in 1997. Within a fortnight the rest of the package was announced: Yamaha engines, Bridgestone tyres and Brazil's Pedro Diniz as number two driver, undoubtedly partly because of the £10 million in sponsorship he carried with him.

Final Battleground

Hill headed for Japan via Hong Kong where he met up with his wife, Georgie, and a couple of friends. They enjoyed a relaxing few days, sight-seeing, even having a night out. Then it was on to the final battleground at Suzuka, 300 miles west of Tokyo in an industrial conglomeration, an ugly, sprawling mess of factories, refineries, garages and storage depots, an employment minister's dream. Pretty it is not, but Hill's only sight was on the world title.

Villeneuve was also in relaxed mood and it started amicably, with assurances that what took place in the way of a world championship would be honourable in the finest of Japanese traditions, like Sumo wrestling, only faster.

'You do not need to hate someone on the track. We have always had good battles on the track and the best battles happen when there is no hate,' said Villeneuve.

'All you will be thinking about is destroying the other guy instead of thinking about what you should be doing. You waste a lot of energy doing that. Damon has had a very good season so there is nothing wrong in him winning it. He has worked hard on his car for years and it is all the work you do that pays you back.'

Yet, in his matter-of-fact way, Villeneuve had a little dig in the ribs when he added: 'If he doesn't win – so, tough.'

Hill was calm and cool, saying: 'There is always pressure on drivers, it just depends how he views it. Jacques may feel that it is a lot of pressure to have to win the race which is what he has to do to have a chance of the championship.

'Throughout the season I have maintained my lead in the championship and I still lead by nine points. The pressure is on Jacques – at least I have other options than just winning.

'The thing for me is that I know I can be world champion on Sunday which is a motivating factor, not pressure.'

Suggestions of team preference for one driver – mainly Villeneuve, as a championship for him would keep the number one on a Williams car – were scorned as much as off-track tricks or driving one another off the track were dismissed. The closest we got was when Hill said with a smile that he would be praying before the start that if anyone broke down, please make sure it was the other guy. 'Not me because there is nothing that can be done about that.'

If he was looking for emotional support from Frank Williams, although that was almost certainly not expected, he had to look hard for when the team owner appeared at the Friday Five session he declined to say Hill deserved the title, insisting it would not be right when his other driver, Jacques Villeneuve, was also going for the title.

'I would agree it would be nice for Damon to win,' said Williams eventually. Would he give an emotional input to his answer? 'No,' he replied.

He did concede: 'Damon has matured very nicely over four years. He has won seven races this year and is a winner. I think Tom has a very nice product coming his way.'

Renault motorsport president, Patrick Faure, had given Hill a pre-race boost by saying that he would have preferred it if Williams had kept Hill for the French company's final year in F1. 'I am sorry you are leaving, good luck in the race,' was Faure's message to Hill.

Williams admitted that it was not his idea to spend '£20,000–£40,000' to guarantee fair play between his two drivers by bringing a fourth car to Suzuka to avoid a clash over who would use the spare car in an emergency. Patrick Head and car designer Adrian Newey, who had hoped not to travel to Japan but to work on the new car for next year, also felt obliged to make the trip to ensure fair play.

'This is the most crucial race of my life and I am ready for it,' said Hill, who was insistent that there would be no preference for either driver from the team. 'It will be the last time I drive a Williams car, certainly for the foreseeable future, and it will be poignant.'

Hill stocked up early with champagne by collecting a jeroboam of bubbly from Moët and Chandon after winning their Silver Trophy for the most victories this season. He had finished Friday's free practice sessions in fifth place behind his title rival, Jacques Villeneuve, but the three-tenths of a second mattered little to the Englishman, who was relaxed about his performance.

The big debate for everyone, not least Hill, was about how

he should tackle the race. He could either attack to win, as some suggested, or just go round in a comfortable sixth place to secure the point he required. The big wheel in the Suzuka circuit funfair kept on spinning and so did Hill's mind as he approached the defining race of his career. He had to admit: 'Right now, I have not made up my mind what I am going to do.

'I am a racing driver and I want to win the race. There would be no better way of winning the championship in the final race than with a victory. That would be the perfect result, the perfect end. In some ways there is more to be said for that and it would be tempting to do it.'

But there was more to it than simply winning for just as the drivers all stood around daring each other to take a chance on the more stomach-churning rides in the fun park, Hill would have loved to take the ultimate in daredevil risks to silence those who had goaded and criticised.

'Going for a win is the most enjoyable way to drive,' he said as he watched the mechanics piece together his Williams car in the garage of an already busy circuit. 'I cannot deny that there is something inside that likes to silence the critics because I like to prove myself and I don't like anyone taking something away from my achievements.

'To win the race would mean there was no way anyone could take anything away from the championship.

'It would be nice to do it completely but I suppose if I were to roll in sixth, no one would remember it ten minutes later. I certainly have to take into account that winning the championship is paramount to me.

'On balance, to win another race [his eighth of the season] would be great . . . but not as great as winning a championship.

'I have to weigh up in my mind whether I want to take more risks with a view to winning the race or to ensure I finish in the points to win the championship. If I am running in the points, I would be very, very happy and I would concentrate on finishing there – that's all I have to do.'

On a soaking Saturday, Hill waited late in the qualifying session before launching his final assault on the grid positions to pull himself up from fifth to second, alongside Villeneuve who dominated the period. Hill was satisfied, he declared, exactly where he wanted to be. It would give him a chance to beat his team-mate into the first corner, he said, as they sat together at the press conference after qualifying.

Yet midway through a sentence, the real tension surfaced when Villeneuve and Schumacher began their by now regular double act which had gone on for several races, striking up an animated conversation as Hill talked. Hill stopped and said: 'Hold on, they're at it again, talking. Pay attention, boys, you might learn something.'

Schumacher, as quick off the track as on it, immediately replied: 'Ok, grandpa.'

Hill later: 'It was pretty lame. It is bad manners and should be stamped out.'

Nearby stood testament to his good nature: 17-year-old William Taylor, a Northamptonshire lad who had been at most of Hill's Silverstone test sessions in all weathers, waving his Union Jack bearing the driver's name. He had gone to the Portuguese Grand Prix, hoping to see Hill win the title, and then stayed on for the test where he had met his hero again. No, he could not afford to go to Japan, he told Hill, and thought no more of it until four days before Suzuka. Brigitte Hill, Damon's sister, telephoned to say that her brother had paid for a return ticket and hotel accommodation and, 48 hours later, William was standing alongside Hill in the paddock.

All day the rain cascaded and although Hill and Villeneuve both said they would prefer a dry race, the general feeling was that Hill would have more of a chance on a wet track for, in 1994, he had won in a monsoon with an outstanding display at Suzuka.

Championship day dawned dry, bright and sunny despite the forecast and Hill was in early from the hotel, situated only 800 yards from the paddock. In warm-up he was fourth, Villeneuve again taking first. The French-Canadian had been unbeatable all weekend but, as he admitted, these were little battles. The big one was still to come.

Perfect Day

The view was as heady as the champagne which washed over him for as Damon Hill gazed out across the crowd, at last his vision was from the top of the world and the glorious sight had freed him. Suddenly he had shaken off the labels: son of double world champion Graham, runner-up, decent loser, too nice, Schumacher's fall guy. Ladies and gentlemen, the 1996 world drivers' champion, Damon Hill. After 13 years, five of them in Formula One, the words swept over him, releasing him from the past, unlocking the door to the Land of New Respect.

'It is fantastic, like being on a rocket that is about to take off,' he declared. 'I have a sense of relief, satisfaction, achievement.' He then began to thank everyone from mechanics to his mother, and especially his wife Georgie and the fans, represented by the fortunate William Taylor. His entourage included friends who had been with him since he was a struggling motorbike rider. Now they could all enjoy being part of his success.

The clock showed 2.45 p.m. as Hill crossed the line in Suzuka but he measured the time in terms of his long struggle and the nurturing of a dream which he had refused to be crushed by critics, doubters and rivals. He had sat in the Williams number five car for the final time for a brief few seconds extra when he arrived back to the *parc fermé* where the cars are scrutinised after races.

His fans waited, his wife waited, but he savoured the moment and private memories flooded his mind. Perhaps those of being around when his father Graham lifted the same world trophy in 1962 and 1968, perhaps the history of being the first son of an F1 champion to emulate that deed, perhaps just surviving to enjoy the moment in a sport which at times demands the ultimate price.

The crown had been officially his 28 minutes earlier. At that moment his only rival, team-mate Jacques Villeneuve, looked in horror as his right rear wheel overtook him at 130 mph and flew into a fence as his global challenge ended in a gravel trap.

Williams would investigate what caused the wheel to work loose and escape but Villeneuve was philosophical and delighted that he had not injured anyone after it leapt a 20-foot fence. 'We did not lose the title in the last race, we screwed up in a few others,' he said.

The news had been relayed immediately to Hill . . . there was no response. He could have pulled over, eased off his charge in first place, but as he explained later: 'The job was not done. It was no time to celebrate.' Even when he flashed past a giant screen and saw Villeneuve standing without his helmet near the wreckage of his car, Hill put the brake on his imagination and kept his foot on concentration.

At last the tensions, the anxieties, the training and testing and sleepless nights were worthwhile. And he had won with dignity, honour and style, putting his name on the trophy with a victory, not a fail-safe drive like a learner driver in a busy high street. The only respite he gave himself was one lap from the end when he swung across to the pitlane crew as he came down the start–finish straight, just to remind them to prepare for his triumphant arrival.

They were ready, and when he next arrived his wife Georgie was fighting back tears of joy, holding a notice which read 'Damon Hill World Champion 1996' and at last his escape to freedom could begin. Did they have another notice saying something different? he was asked minutes later. 'Williams are always prepared,' said Hill with a laugh.

By then he was a walking champagne bottle, thoroughly soaked by Schumacher and third placed Mika Hakkinen who baptised him as champion by total immersion.

'Get a wetsuit and have some aspirins,' was Schumacher's advice about the celebrations to come. 'You deserve the title.' And with that the two men who have sniped at each other, collided and crashed, shook hands.

His 16th step to the title in the Japanese Grand Prix had been largely incident-free but the start had been delayed for ten minutes when former team-mate David Coulthard's car stalled just as the final light was about to launch the cars off the grid. Would it prove too much for Hill's nerves to take, would he suffer another of the lumbering starts which had plagued his recent races?

Hill answered the doubters, ice-cool in the soaring heat of the early afternoon. Villeneuve was being swallowed up as his wheels spun impotently and, from pole position, he reached the first corner sixth. Hill, who needed only to finish in the top six while Villeneuve had to be first *and* hope that his rival failed to score a point, was gone, heading up to the summit of achievement.

He was never headed and rarely troubled after shutting the door firmly on Gerhard Berger on the third lap when the Austrian broke a front wing ambitiously attempting to dive inside Hill. Two pit-stops were faultless and he kept his cool until 30 seconds from the end when he erupted on the car radio, shouting his thanks to the team for their work, their help and how wonderful they were.

'The race win was for them, the championship was for me,' said Hill in a quieter moment sometime later. 'To be honest, it had to be this year for me and I am really, really delighted. Winning the championship is the hardest thing I have ever done.

'It was the perfect race, the perfect day. People talk about feelings but you don't allow them during the race. I just thought that I had a great start and a good opportunity to stay ahead but I kept my eye on Jacques.

'I just had to maintain the gap on second place and I was able to drive within my limits, without too many risks, and stay ahead.

'The chequered flag was a beautiful moment. In that moment I was allowed to let go, to start to congratulate myself instead of concentrating on what had to be done.'

He headed for the Williams offices soon after and called in to see Frank Williams, the man who had discarded him. Forever the team player, Hill thanked him and at last got the compliment he never believed would come.

'He told the team it was a pleasure working with them all,'

said Williams. 'I don't know if he included me in that.

'I told him he fully deserved the title. He won superbly this year and was the best man out there. He has had an exemplary career so far and fully deserves that he got what he wanted. He could so easily do it again, no doubt about that. This year he has been very masterful in the car.'

Hill paid tribute to the team, saying: 'It has been an absolutely brilliant season with eight wins. The team has not put a foot wrong in my view and I am sorry to be leaving . . . but what a way to leave.'

If the road ahead had been difficult to see at times, now Hill knew exactly where he was bound. It is easier from the top of the world.

Georgie Hill had watched her husband crowned and they had a long hug when he finally stopped, but she missed most of his glory race – she had buried her head in a towel because of the tension. As she watched him in the packed press conference, he dedicated the race to her, saying: 'She gave me the strength I needed to see it through. She is fantastic.'

Georgie was thrilled but returned the compliment and the race. 'He told me he was giving me the championship but I am giving it back to him. He deserves it, he did all the hard work, took the strain and made lots of sacrifices. He stuck totally to his dream and slogged his guts out to get there. He started from nothing. He was a £40-a-week van driver and despatch rider.

'At no point did I ever feel he would not do it and I have always been certain that one day he would be crowned world champion.'

Later that night came strange scenes. Hill grabbed Michael Schumacher – whose two-year reign he had ended – and they leaned into the microphone and bawled the chorus to Queen's 'We Are The Champions', and the packed log cabin looked set to burst as the audience roared with delight. Songs for every occasion were reeled out on the karaoke video and soon Hill was back on the floor with Georgie who joined him in a soulful rendition of 'My Way'.

Nearby, David Coulthard and Jacques Villeneuve stood ready to join in for 'Dancing Queen' but the two drivers were now completely shaven-headed, having accepted the challenge to go for a new look, the expert tonsorial touch being supplied by Villeneuve's Scottish manager Craig Pollock. Schumacher fans arrived and were soon chorusing along to a spoof version of the *Dad's Army* theme tune as a group of Hill's friends who had flown over for the race sang 'Who do you think you are kidding, Schumacher?'

The final night of the Formula One season and the rejoicing for Hill proved a potent force in the little karaoke cabins behind the circuit hotel where the guests can have a party. No one parties like Grand Prix guests.

Earlier, hotel residents had been treated to another bizarre sight as Hill arrived back from his race victory only to find a huge crowd of autograph hunters waiting. He drove straight through and into the hotel lobby to avoid another bruising from the overeager fans. He had set off on his moped in the dark in heavy rain and decided to have one last victory roll around the circuit but confessed: 'It was just too slow. We turned back and headed for the hotel. When I saw the crowds, I just rode into the lobby.'

That was the start of the big night but Hill left before many of the revellers. At 4 a.m., as some were still making their way home, he was unable to sleep any more and rose to take a silent walk in the hotel grounds, able for the first time to enjoy the company of his own thoughts and dwell on what he had achieved.

A few hours later, he was travelling at 160 mph again, shaking off the effects of a heavy night and his singalong-a-Schumacher. He was glancing at the Japanese newspapers as he hurtled along, sipping a cup of coffee. Not that being world drivers' champion had made him blasé. He had simply decided to travel by the most suitable vehicle for his new status: the world's fastest ground transport. In the famed Shinkansen, the Bullet Train, he covered the 280 miles to Tokyo in just under two hours to fulfil commitments.

'My mind has been so tied up with what might happen and concentrating on what had to be done. Now that I don't need to do that any more, it is like a massive release. It is as if the brake is off on my brain and now suddenly I can relax for the first time in a long while,' said Hill.

The Bullet shot past Mount Fuji but Hill had climbed his own mountain. He was ready for the challenge of another with Arrows but, for the moment, he was content to gaze from on high and delight in the view, at last recognised as a hero in his own land.

Race 16: Japanese Grand Prix

Result	Drivers (overall)	Constructors (overall)
1. Damon Hill (GB)	1. Hill 97	1. Williams 175
2. Michael Schumacher (Ger)	2. Villeneuve 78	2. Ferrari 70
3. Mika Hakkinen (Fin)	3. Schumacher 59	3. Benetton 68
4. Gerhard Berger (Aut)		
5. Martin Brundle (GB)		
6. Heinz-Harald Frentzen (Ger)		

The Daily Express

HOW TO WIN ON THE HORSES

DANNY HALL

The renowned *Daily Express* racing team show you how you can make your horse racing pay

- New edition – completely revised with updated statistics

- Studying form – there's no substitute

- In the ring – how to get value

- At the track – what to look for in the paddock

- Race-reading – how to spot non triers

- Ante-post betting – pitfalls and profits

- Results section – winning patterns in the last ten years

'Danny Hall has done a superb job in producing a cogently written and info-packed punters' guide'
Odds On

Here is everything you need to know to beat the bookies!

NON-FICTION / SPORT 0 7472 4444 8

Stephen F. Kelly

NOT JUST A GAME

The Book For Every Football Fan

Drugs, under-the-table payments, allegations of match-fixing, English fans rioting in Ireland *et l'affaire* Cantona. These were just a few of the events from a sensational 1994–95 soccer season. What's more, there was the football as well, including a little competition across the Atlantic called the World Cup. It's all here in this first ever anthology of a season – the finest football writing of the year.

Read All About It!

Baggio's tears, Cantona's stud marks, the Toon Army, the £7 million man and Sir Stan at eighty. There's all this, plus lots more, in a dazzling collection to be savoured over the next twelve months.

NON-FICTION / SPORT 0 7472 4983 0

My Old Man and the Sea

DAVID HAYES and DANIEL HAYES

Some fathers and sons go fishing together. David and Daniel Hayes decided to sail a tiny boat 17,000 miles to the bottom of the world and back. This is their story.

David, the father, is romantic, excitable and reflective; Daniel is wry, comic and down to earth. On the voyage, the father relinquishes control and the son becomes captain. Together, their alternate voices weave a story of travel, adventure and difficult, sometimes terrifying sailing. Soon they are headed for the huge waves and unceasing winds of the Southern Ocean, with only their skill as sailors, a compass, a sextant, a ship's cat named Tiger and *Sparrow*, the 25-foot boat they've built together.

The Caribbean, the Panama Canal, the Galapagos Islands, Easter Island, Cape Horn, the Falklands – these far-flung places spring vividly to life. Lovers of sailing and travel books will find it hard to forget this hilarious and often moving tale of voyage and self-discovery. *My Old Man and the Sea* has already been a bestseller in America, and is to be made into a film by Steven Spielberg.

'One of the most beautiful and intricate portrayals of the father/son relationship that I have encountered' Christopher Hudson, *Daily Mail*

'The best-written, most vivid and thoughtful sailing narrative in decades' Jonathan Raban, *Observer*

NON-FICTION / TRAVEL 0 7472 5467 2

A selection of non-fiction from Headline

THE NEXT 500 YEARS	Adrian Berry	£7.99	☐
FIGHT FOR THE TIGER	Michael Day	£7.99	☐
LEFT FOOT FORWARD	Garry Nelson	£5.99	☐
THE NATWEST PLAYFAIR CRICKET ANNUAL	Bill Frindall	£4.99	☐
THE JACK THE RIPPER A–Z	Paul Begg, Martin Fido & Keith Skinner	£8.99	☐
VEGETARIAN GRUB ON A GRANT	Cas Clarke	£5.99	☐
PURE FRED	Rupert Fawcett	£6.99	☐
THE SUPERNATURAL A–Z	James Randi	£6.99	☐
ERIC CANTONA: MY STORY	Eric Cantona	£6.99	☐
THE TRUTH IN THE LIGHT	Peter and Elizabeth Fenwick	£6.99	☐
GOODBYE BAFANA	James Gregory	£6.99	☐
MY OLD MAN AND THE SEA	Daniel Hayes and David Hayes	£5.99	☐

All Headline books are available at your local bookshop or newsagent, or can be ordered direct from the publisher. Just tick the titles you want and fill in the form below. Prices and availability subject to change without notice.

Headline Book Publishing, Cash Sales Department, Bookpoint, 39 Milton Park, Abingdon, OXON, OX14 4TD, UK. If you have a credit card you may order by telephone – 01235 400400.

Please enclose a cheque or postal order made payable to Bookpoint Ltd to the value of the cover price and allow the following for postage and packing:

UK & BFPO: £1.00 for the first book, 50p for the second book and 30p for each additional book ordered up to a maximum charge of £3.00.
OVERSEAS & EIRE: £2.00 for the first book, £1.00 for the second book and 50p for each additional book.

Name ....

Address ....

....

....

If you would prefer to pay by credit card, please complete:
Please debit my Visa/Access/Diner's Card/American Express (delete as applicable) card no:

Signature .... Expiry Date ....

PENGUIN BOOKS

THE GIRLS' GUIDE TO
HUNTING AND FISHING

'Witty, sharp, funny and sincere' *Daily Mirror*

'A refreshing rarity: an intelligent page-turner . . . a delicate
and carefully crafted classic novel' *Express*

'Thoroughly engaging' *Financial Times*

'Some books get buzz, and *The Girls' Guide* has had more
buzz than a swarm of bees . . . what is unusual for a first
book is the emotional truth Bank manages to capture as she
traces Jane's progress' *Times Metro*

'Tagged the thinking woman's Helen Fielding . . . a
beautifully written and very funny novel . . . as with
Salinger and Carver, there is a crystalline simplicity to
Bank's prose' *Guardian*

'There is a humour, a kind of kooky oddness to her writing
and her characters, that is all her own, and it is this which
should ensure that both book and author will crop up again
and again this summer and beyond' *Irish Times*

'Mix Helen Fielding with J. D. Salinger, add Jane's soul and
you have the essence of *Girls' Guide* – blissful brilliance'
She

'This is the most enchanting and refreshing book I have
read all summer' Amanda Craig, *Jewish Chronicle*

Melissa Bank has had several stories published in US magazines. An international bestseller, *The Girls' Guide to Hunting and Fishing* is her first book and has been published in twenty-one countries.